THE
ORACLE
EDGE

**How Oracle Corporation's
Take No Prisoners Strategy
Has Created an
$8 Billion Software Powerhouse**

by
Stuart Read

ADAMS MEDIA CORPORATION
Holbrook, Massachusetts

Published by
Adams Media Corporation
260 Center Street, Holbrook, MA 02343

ISBN: 1-58062-165-1

Printed in the United States of America

J I H G F E D C B A

Library of Congress Cataloging-in-Publication Data

The Oracle edge: how Oracle Corporation's take no prisoners strategy
has created an $8 billion software powerhouse / by Stuart Read.
p.   cm.
ISBN 1-58062-165-1
Includes index.
1. Oracle Corporation—History. 2. Ellison, Larry. 3. Computer software industry—
United States—History. 4. Businessmen—United States—Biography. I. Title.
HD9696.63.U640727   1999
338.7'610053'0973—dc21   99-35387
CIP

Cover photo courtesy of Oracle Corporation

*This book is available at quantity discounts for bulk purchases.
For information, call 1-800-872-5627.*

Visit our home page at http://www.businesstown.com

Contents

Acknowledgments .... **ix**

Chapter 1
Introduction **1**

Chapter 2
Company Character **7**
Build a Company with "Leadership Pull" and
   "Cultural Push"............................. 9
Image Matters: Dress for Success 10
Create Excitement about Your Business 18

Chapter 3
Corporate Strategy **23**
Eat Your Own Dog Food (Use Your Own Products) . . 26
Implement Systems Using Your Software 26
Build Brand One Word at a Time 30
Grow Without Acquisition—The Oracle Way........ 31
Locate Your International Headquarters Internationally. . 34
Be First in a New Market and Dominate It.......... 37
Balance Development and Sales 39
Foster Entrepreneurship Within 41
Drive Productivity with Competition, Not Chaos 45
Make Your Enemies' Enemy Your Friend 48

Chapter 4

Product Development **51**

Develop for the "Built-in Consumer"............. 54

Make Your Product Strategic to the Customer 56

Build with Failure in Mind 61

Whatever You Do—Ship!........................ 64

Anticipate the Next Wave....................... 65

Nurture Your Core Team....................... 67

Permeate Your Organization with Information 71

Chapter 5

Incredible Selling Power **75**

Build Incentives that Get Sales' Attention........... 78

Create Infrastructure that Supports
      Revenue Generation 81

Go Straight to the Top 86

Marketing to Enterprise Customers—
      Seminar Power!........................... 90

Sell into Vertical Industries 93

Sales Today Make Markets Tomorrow.............. 96

Promote Your Vision 100

Chapter 6

Customer Relationships **103**

Visit Your Customers........................... 105

Talk with Your Customers 107

Watch Your Customers Use Your Product.......... 108

Help Customers Use Your Product................ 109

Set Realistic Expectations....................... 116

Chapter 7

Crush Your Competition **119**

Five Steps to Attacking Your Competition.......... 121

Cut Off the Oxygen............................ 122

Pigeonholing Individual Competitors 124
Document Victories 128
Fight Opponents on Your Terms 130
Deploy the Advertising Weapon 133
Lock Customers In and Competitors Out 138

Chapter 8
Talent **141**
Recruit Athletes 143
Indoctrinate with Company Culture 150
Communicate Your "Mantra" 156

Chapter 9
Management Philosophy **159**
Teach People How to Win 161
Give Power to Individuals and Teams 163
Spend Money on what Matters 166
Make a Commitment; Keep It 167
Think Like a Shareholder 169
Be an Accessible Manager 170
Spoil the Best Employees 171
Don't Be Afraid to Terminate 173
Shake Up Your Organization 175
See Opportunity in Change 179

Chapter 10
Surviving a "Crash" **181**
Identify Crucial Issues 184
Turn the Company Around 186
Learn the Hard Lessons 190
Fix Weaknesses and Forge Ahead 191

Chapter 11

Exploring New Markets **193**

Dreaming of Interactive Television 196

Taking on Microsoft with the Network Computer . . . 200

Eliminating the Competition from Your Deals 201

Lessons Learned from the Network Computer. 204

Chapter 12

The All or Nothing Future **215**

The Inevitable Clash 217

Understanding Microsoft's Strengths 221

Evaluating Oracle's Strengths 223

Finding Strategies that Amplify Oracle's Advantages. . 226

Forging Partnerships 233

Honing the Edge 235

Index **237**

Acknowledgments

THERE ARE TENS OF THOUSANDS OF PEOPLE WHO CONTRIBUTED TO THE STORY OF ORACLE, AND CONSEQUENTLY TO THIS BOOK. Among them there is a select group that I would like to thank for spending time with me to look back at the battles that Oracle has fought and the things that Oracle has accomplished:

Bob Berger, Arnold Blinn, Roy Bukstein, Kaui Demarzo, Randy Dieterle, Joe Gillach, Bruce Kasrel, Paul King, John Landwehr, Andy Laursen, Ben Linder, Paige Mazzoni, Bruce Mitchell, Mark Moore, Laura Pickering, Mark Porter, Cindy Taylor, Smokey Wallace, and Chuck Weiss.

I also want to express my gratitude to Karen Logsdon for her tireless editing and creative hours spent helping me convert raw words into a smooth story. And finally, I am most appreciative of my wife Teri's support through the trials of my first book.

Thank you all.

CHAPTER ONE

Introduction

WALL STREET INVESTORS, SILICON VALLEY JUNKIES, AND AVID COMPUTER USERS ALIKE HAVE MARVELED AT THE SUCCESS AND GROWTH OF ORACLE CORPORATION. Although it may not be a household name like Microsoft or Apple Computer, in fewer than twenty years, Oracle has grown to 41,000 employees worldwide. With offices in more than 140 countries—from Canada to Kazakhstan—Oracle's revenues are expected to top $8 billion in 1999, helping the company to maintain its position as the second largest independent software company in the world.

Today, two-thirds of the Fortune 100 companies use Oracle software somewhere in their organization. With products available on more than ninety different computing platforms and installations across the globe, it is safe to say that Oracle touches the lives of nearly every businessperson. When an individual is searching inventory lists, reviewing customer requests, or getting money from an ATM machine, Oracle's relational database is probably at work.

Universality was certainly part of the vision for Larry Ellison and his partners who cofounded the company in 1979 and later named it Oracle. Among the Greeks and Romans, the "oracle" was a person of great knowledge or wisdom. The oracle was the person to whom everyone else went for answers. When it comes to information management, businesses still come to Oracle.

Like many high-technology companies, Oracle began as a consulting project. Larry Ellison and others were tasked with building a proprietary database on an Amdahl mainframe computer for the Air Force. But instead of creating a whole new database architecture from scratch, they discovered a recently published research document (Dr. E. F. Codd, "A Relational Model of Data for Large Shared Data Banks," *Communications of the Association of Computing Machinery* 13 (6): 377-387 (1970).) and used it as the foundation for their project. The Codd document described the relational database model and the accompanying SQL (stands for Structured Query Language and is pronounced "sequel") language. Using that and an IBM specification for relational database management (called "System R") as their basis, Ellison and his partners built the first commercial relational database.

Once the product was created, the Oracle team surveyed the market for its database software and found it consisted only of businesses that owned machines made by Amdahl, Larry Ellison's former employer. While Amdahl was doing well at the time, there were many other types of computers in use, and Oracle didn't have compatible software for any of them.

Larry Ellison sensed opportunity. If a company, or better yet, HIS company, could solve the technical problems that would allow Oracle software to run on any computer, Oracle could make the choice of computer platform irrelevant. And more importantly, Oracle would be able to deliver peace of mind to customers while establishing a competitive advantage for the both the customer and Oracle. Part luck, part vision: Oracle's founders stumbled into Information Management, an industry with untold market demand, and found that the Oracle database could be its foundation.

At the heart of every inventory system, every automated teller machine, and every international export is a central store of information, a database. Before Oracle, electronic databases were so difficult to use that only wealthy companies could afford the large teams of programmers necessary to write and maintain them. But Oracle changed all that with its relational database model, which organizes information neatly into tables of rows and columns, provides a standard database access language (SQL), and manages each transaction to ensure data integrity.

Thanks to Oracle, moving from a paper filing system to an electronic database was suddenly realistic for more than just a handful of companies. And the rewards to be gained from having information such as centralized customer and financial records automated were so great that organizations were willing to spend a lot of money for Oracle software. For example, a shipping company that took a week to process a container using the paper system could now use Oracle's software to process shipments in seconds, beating its competition and saving thousands of dollars on every shipment. The immediate returns that companies experienced made it easy to justify spending millions of dollars on Oracle's new database software and the hardware necessary to run it.

The dominant player in the enterprise information management software market, Oracle represents one of a precious few remaining threats to the Microsoft empire today. The cause is Oracle's visionary president, Larry Ellison. As Oracle grew, Larry threw out many of the traditional approaches to managing people and products and created an environment that fostered unbounded growth and success. Along the way, he not only set, but maintained, high standards for himself and his company, standards which enabled Oracle in its first ten years of existence to more than double its revenues each year. Just imagine, investors who bought Oracle stock in 1990 have seen their investment increase fifteen fold over the last eight years. That's a better return than stock from Lotus, Compaq, and even Microsoft!

While it may appear that Oracle's history is too much like a business fairy tale, its success may serve as the ultimate case study for those searching for explosive growth in their own businesses or careers. In this book, the basic philosophy behind Oracle's success will be boiled down to individual rules, applicable to anyone in any business.

Oracle's techniques for building company character and corporate strategy, developing products, creating intense selling power, and staying in touch with customers contain valuable lessons for fostering growth, while Larry Ellison's Genghis Khan-inspired assaults on the competition give insight into how one survives in the new hyper-competitive global environment. For Ellison, any business tolerant of a competitor is doomed, and any business comfortable with being second will end up being last!

In the next eleven chapters, you will discover the unique strategies that Oracle has employed to deliver exciting technology, create explosive revenue growth, demolish the competition, win over customers, inspire employees, and steer the company to the commanding spot it enjoys in the high-technology marketplace.

The lessons learned from Oracle can give your business the Edge!

CHAPTER TWO

Company
Character

The very fact that Oracle people think they have a unique culture is an indicator of what that culture is like. It is full of people who think they are special.

—ORACLE MARKETING VETERAN

Build a Company with "Leadership Pull" and "Cultural Push"

ONE OF THE AMAZING THINGS ABOUT ORACLE IS HOW WELL IT HAS SURVIVED IN AN EXTREMELY COMPETITIVE ENVIRONMENT THAT IS CHANGING RAPIDLY. The past twenty years have brought a series of challenges to the company that have required incisive and strategic action. At the highest level, Oracle has survived and thrived under these conditions because it has both strong leadership and a culture that drives employees to succeed.

Larry Ellison brings leadership to the company. He actively involves himself in large and small issues, touching every area of the company. Having a single navigator has made it easier for Oracle to cut through bureaucracy to make critical decisions swiftly, even as the company grew past ten thousand and twenty thousand employees. Having a person who is a single focal point creates a company that can change and adapt to shifting market demands and sudden competitive threats more quickly than hierarchical or committee-driven companies. Having a single focus also helps a company to grow faster. It is easier to get employees aligned with a new approach if there's a highly visible, committed, motivated leader who can provide a model for them to follow. Larry Ellison steps out and pulls others along. The result is an organization that focuses on the high-priority, high payoff projects as Larry defines them. He makes things happen.

Larry Ellison also brings a culture to the company. Many of the tactics that Oracle uses—crush the competition, grow quickly, and think strategically—are reflected in elements of Ellison's own personality, elements that he has amplified over time to bring focus to the company's critical success factors and set a high standard for employees. This section will examine some of the unique attributes of Oracle culture, explain how Larry Ellison has created and animated them, and how that benefits the company. To understand Oracle, one must understand Larry Ellison. In the fast-moving, fast-paced computer industry, Oracle has achieved success because of Larry's style, where image matters and only the best is good enough.

Image Matters: Dress for Success

In my six years at Oracle, I never saw Larry Ellison in a T-shirt. Unlike his friend, Steve Jobs, who regularly dresses in a black turtleneck and jeans, Larry typically wears tailored Italian suits and ties, and he wears them with panache. Larry's wardrobe sets the standard for the way his employees dress. Every field salesperson maintains a similar look. Double-breasted suits are a favorite and ties have a maximum working life of about nine months. Even the telesales force, which only interacts with customers over the telephone, is stylishly attired in crisp white shirts, Bally loafers, and Christian Dior suits.

Larry places a premium on image and most people who work at Oracle follow suit. It's hard to find a stereotypical nerd at Oracle. Most employees don't wear thick glasses, rumpled shirts, or high-water pants. In general, Oracle employees are presentable and are in good physical shape. Having hosted a large number of customers and partners to Oracle headquarters, I know that it is something that makes a strong positive impression on anyone who comes into contact with the company.

Adopt icons with relevant and positive associations

Ellison has long had an appreciation for Japanese art and culture. His home resembles a traditional Japanese building and is decorated inside with an exotic array of Japanese antiques. He has even taken the time to learn spoken Japanese. Ellison's explorations of Japanese culture seem closely related to his admiration for and emulation of the ancient Japanese samurai warriors. The characterization applies in many areas, as he relies on rigorous training and innovative strategy—both hallmarks of the ancient samurai. The characterization gives both outsiders and employees another positive icon to associate with Oracle and with Ellison himself.

Project a positive perception

Long before Oracle built the glamorous glass buildings in Redwood Shores and before the company was even called Oracle, the initial staff occupied a small suite of offices on Sand Hill Road in Menlo Park. Sand Hill Road is known in Silicon Valley as the home of the venture capital (VC) community. Many of the VCs keep extra office space on

Sand Hill Road that they use to incubate tiny companies before those companies are ready for large amounts of funding or their own offices. Desperate to make good on the product promises that Larry had made, the original Oracle team stayed late night after night in its Sand Hill office suite, coding the early implementation of Oracle software. On many of those nights, a particular venture capitalist on Sand Hill Road was also working late. Already a prominent member of the venture community, this person was on his way out the door well after normal business hours and noticed that the lights were still on in the suite occupied by Larry and his team. The lights always seemed to be on and the activity constant in the Oracle suite. It caught his attention. Anyone that dedicated had to be onto something interesting. The rest is history. He was one of the original and few external funders of Oracle Corporation and is still actively involved with the company.

A VC friend of mine has a metric he calls the "parking lot test." If he's interested in a company, he'll drive by the parking lot, late on a weeknight or on a Saturday afternoon, just to see how many cars are there. Using that test, he says he can determine whether the people in the company really have a vision or if they are in it just for a paycheck. He invests in vision. The point is not to make all your employees work every hour of every day or to fill the parking lot with old cars so that people will think that there is perpetual activity, but to understand that your organization is always under scrutiny. You never know what key investors or customers will look at or when they will choose to look at it. Make sure that when someone looks at the company from the outside, they see what you want them to see. Looking at your own company as if from the outside is important to understand how the organization is perceived and is an interesting way to gauge your own success in establishing a vision and an urgency. Even though it's a large company now, the hard work ethic still remains at Oracle. I drove by its parking lot at about 8 P.M. last week and there were still a large number of cars in the parking lot.

Communicate success

When I was hired by Oracle, I was a student at Harvard University. Part of my Oracle offer included a relocation package. Unlike most people who elected to use their relocation money to have professional movers pack their things and transport them, I chose to pack and move myself so I could use the money for a leisurely trip across the country. I drove with a classmate from Harvard who was starting at Oracle at the same time I was. When we arrived in San Francisco, we had enjoyed a great trip, but we were virtually out of money. With the limited funds we had remaining, we checked into a seedy motel in San Mateo by the side of Highway 101. We then proceeded to Oracle to let the new-hire ambassador, know that we had arrived and to find out what to do next. When she found out where we were staying, she was visibly upset. "You're Oracle people now, and Oracle people stay in nice places!" She promptly moved us into a hotel that cost eight times what we were paying. We understood instantly. We were now part of a successful company and had to live up to the image of success.

Design with style

By the late 1980s, Oracle had outgrown its original campus on Davis Drive in Belmont. A new and befitting compound had to be built to house one of the fastest growing companies in Silicon Valley. Oracle bought a parcel of land in Redwood Shores and retained a famous architect who planned the design for the new campus. The single direction Larry gave was that he wanted, "a gleaming monolith in a Japanese garden." The buildings, designed primarily of green glass, together form a cold but elegant icon of a futuristic corporation.

Around the buildings, all of the Oracle grounds are meticulously cared for and the plantings are often changed by season. In front of 500 Oracle Parkway, which houses Larry Ellison's office, the landscaping is of particular interest. The winter brings a rock garden, composed of almost identical round black stones, all raked to make a particular pattern. In the spring, there is Japanese bamboo, and so on.

Inside the buildings, Larry has made sure that Oracle is decorated with original art. While not all Japanese, much of the art is museum-quality and is circulated so the employees don't always have to see the same works. Larry has made a concerted effort to bring culture and style to every Oracle employees' life. An ex-Oracle employee told me, "It is just amazing, I need to run an errand to drop something off at Oracle and my husband wants to come with me to see the place. People are really intrigued by and drawn to this company."

The elegance of the campus pays off for Oracle in a number of tangible ways. Not only is it an impressive sign of the company's success to customers and partners who come to visit, it is also a strong motivator to people who work there. People are willing to go to work earlier and stay there longer because they work in a nice setting. People also work harder to achieve the level of accomplishment that is associated with the company's obvious goals and successes. And finally, it is a powerful recruiting tool for attracting top talent into Oracle.

Create an environment that embraces interaction and teamwork

One of the most popular buildings in the Oracle complex is a gleaming two-story fitness center. The facility is equipped with an Olympic-sized pool, aerobics studios, full basketball court, workout room with every kind of machine imaginable, and even a sand volleyball court. The fitness center was being built just as Oracle entered some difficult financial times, and the effort drew a great deal of criticism. It was common knowledge that the fitness center effort was costing in excess of $10 million. But Larry pressed on, believing that employee fitness was important and, perhaps more importantly, wanting to show all the world what Oracle had. Today, the fitness center is truly an Oracle icon, featuring fit, energetic employees all dressed up, sweating and schmoozing with their peers. Oracle employees can also sponsor a spouse or friend for membership to the Oracle fitness center at a bargain rate, an excellent recruiting and personal relations tool.

Another unique aspect of Oracle is the cafeteria in every headquarters building. Throw away any thoughts of a college cafeteria. Each Oracle cafeteria has a cuisine theme and corresponding decor. Expensive hardwoods and stylized stainless steel and glass create the ambiance that one might expect from a restaurant in downtown San Francisco, but employees don't have to leave the Oracle campus. Work continues right through lunch in Oracle's cafeterias. And the food is good! Italian, American, Japanese, French— whatever your pleasure—all are represented, and the cafeterias even offer take-home dinners, encouraging employees to work late.

Be persuasive

Larry makes Oracle hard to refuse, and his power of persuasion is a quality that permeates the company. Oracle's first CFO had the opportunity to see Larry Ellison in a number of different selling situations. About all of them, he said, "I felt sorry for analysts, investment bankers, customers, and prospective employees after they met with Larry. I challenge a customer to turn down an offer from Larry Ellison. I don't know how anyone does it. He is irresistible." That kind of selling makes billion dollar companies!

Stay intense

Larry Ellison has the luxury of dabbling in casual interests outside of work, but he doesn't. When he races his ocean sailboat, *Sayonara*, he is just as driven as he is in the office. One of the people on his team, who has also raced on America's Cup sailboats, says he's, "never seen a skipper who is as intense, as strategic, and as focused as Larry. It is clearly something that is part of his life." Anyone close to Larry Ellison knows that after a long day of work he goes home and answers his e-mail. It is not uncommon to get a response or a note from Larry Ellison sent at 10 P.M. or 11 P.M., and that intensity permeates the entire organization. A development head I spoke with articulated it best: "The schedule here is flexible. You can work any hours you want—but don't kid yourself—it's 60 hours a week."

Seek perfection

Several years ago, after an annual report had already gone to print, Larry decided that he didn't like his quote on the cover. Although all of the pages and the cover had been printed, the book had not yet been bound. In the pursuit of perfection, Larry demanded that the team stop the presses and print new covers. The cost of the exercise was $50,000, but Larry was willing to spend the money to get the annual report right. In the competitive database software market, the reward for "getting it right the first time" is high, and the message to Oracle employees is that perfection is the expectation.

Eliminate mediocrity

Not only does Larry have a strong sense of excellence, but he has also passed it on to the company. Oracle takes it one step further with its genuine intolerance for mediocrity. Superiority starts with the CEO and permeates the organization. "Larry suffers no fools," a vice president told me, and neither does the rest of Oracle. Settling for anything less than great in your organization implies that average is acceptable. Oracle has never been willing to send that message to its employees, and neither should any company with aspirations of success.

Exude perception of ownership

Larry continues to maintain a significant interest in Oracle, and at last count he personally owned more than 20 percent of the outstanding stock. Despite his ownership share of the company, Larry also exudes a personal "perception of ownership" in the company, and it is clear that he is in charge. He has a vision for the future, an active role in product strategy, and the support of the entire organization. Although he is the company's founder, he continually reinforces his own personal impact on the organization by conducting product reviews and addressing the company. His attitude is a positive one for Oracle employees who also feel ownership over their jobs and the responsibility for quality as a result.

Oracle's company culture may seem exaggerated or over-hyped, but having a defined culture makes a big difference in an environment experiencing radical growth. It provides a cohesive way to bring the company together and keep it moving in the right direction. Any fast-paced organization will benefit from having a decisive leader and a strong identity. It gives the employees, press, analysts, investors, and even customers something with which to relate, whether they agree with all the pieces or not. You should take the time to identify the elements of your own corporate culture that you want to develop and amplify and which you choose to sweep under the corporate carpet.

Create Excitement about Your Business

As a company's character is being established, and perhaps even more importantly, when a company's character is already established, it's imperative to maintain an intangible that I call "the Excitement Factor." Oracle, and specifically Larry Ellison, is fantastic at creating the Excitement Factor—over and over again.

The idea is to take a mundane product, a daily task, or an accomplishment and make people understand why it is exciting and important. "I remember always being excited when I was at Oracle," a product manager told me. People at Oracle are excited to be there, and customers get excited when they hear about the latest thing from Oracle.

These are some of the ways that Oracle created and maintains the Excitement Factor:

Retain people by creating new opportunity internally

Oracle creates opportunity internally, then makes people work for it. Success is gratifying if the result is meaningful, and accomplishment means more if it doesn't come easily. This certainly applies to challenging individuals within a company. A product manager told me about her experience at Oracle, "It was such a competitive environment. It totally appealed to my personality." For her, part of the Excitement Factor was competing with other people within the company. At Oracle, she had opportunities to get products out earlier or with fewer bugs, to create new ways of documenting a product, or to make it easier to install. Within the company, she had the opportunity to make an impact, and that furthered her career. When she was successful at doing something better, she gleamed with pride. When someone else had done something extraordinary, the bar was reset and she would work that much harder.

One of the developers who started at the same time I did told me that in his first one-on-one meeting with his new manager, he was told: "You have ownership of 4.5 percent of the core database code. If you can make your code run 10 percent faster, that will translate into bottom-line growth for the company." My classmate related immediately. "Fix code—make money—that was cool." Oracle does a great job of helping employees understand how what they are doing impacts the company as a whole.

Encourage competition externally

Clearly, the excitement of a battle rallies employees—and even customers. Oracle never shied away from waging wars with competitors, whether it was Ingres, Informix, or Sybase. In Chapter 7 you will read details about how employees derived a huge amount of excitement from getting into competition with an opponent, and even more when they beat them. In the heat of specific battles, Oracle handed out T-shirts, awards, and money to employees who fought hard and emerged victorious. Even customers got a charge out of the zeal with which Oracle people would pursue the competition, leaving a market perception that Oracle must have something better if its employees are so eager to take on the competition.

Celebrate success

Throughout the years, Oracle has had great success both in terms of product and financial accomplishments. Unlike many companies, however, Oracle takes the time to make sure that employees and customers alike appreciate what the company has accomplished. Oracle instills a sense of pride and excitement when it comes to the company's achievements, and celebrations ranging from individual recognition to departmental outings are not uncommon. After a big product shipment, the head of Oracle's New Media division took the entire division, with spouses, to Hawaii for a celebration. At the party where Oracle celebrated passing a billion dollars a year in revenue, a coworker turned to me and said, "Wow! We're really part of something big here, aren't we?" We were, and Oracle wanted to make sure that we knew it.

Demonstrate vision

Oracle, specifically Ellison, makes inspiring product announcements. He talks about things that people dream about. That's not always easy to do if you are selling industrial-strength database software, but it's one of the best ways to keep employees and customers excited. Part of the excitement around Oracle's product announcements is that they are generally premature, and as a result, futuristic and visionary. But they have a purpose. They help to maintain the Excitement Factor. For example, at the product announcement in which Larry laid out some of the exciting new video on-demand applications built on Oracle technology, he did a tremendous job at generating enthusiasm despite the fact that everyone knew that it would be years before video on-demand would be a reality. His ideas were revolutionary, inspirational, and bold, but they proved to the audience (employees, press, and analysts) that there was an application out there that made Oracle's core database product more exciting.

Make it relevant

One of the biggest factors in generating excitement is relevance. Larry Ellison is also able to translate lofty ideas into simple terms that get people excited. Why? Because he doesn't talk about common database terms, such as row-level locks or latch technology, he talks about how Oracle's database is going to run on your PC so that you can log in from home and understand your company's information needs from your own study. Oracle figures out what customers want, and its employees use relevant examples to communicate these messages. Oracle knows that in order for you to understand its products, you must understand how they will change your life in some compelling way. Then, Oracle builds a simple real-life example to describe it. "How does this affect me, Al Franken?" a vice president used to ask about a new feature or a new technology, meaning "How does this impact the average person?" Oracle knows how to translate that importance into words that anyone can understand. The idea that you, or something that you are working on, could improve someone else's life is a very powerful concept and is at the heart of the Excitement Factor.

Although the art of creating the Excitement Factor is specific to each company and each individual, two of the most critical elements are the sense of importance and the power of repetition. Make sure every employee understands why a particular product or task is important to the person on the street, and once that product or task is understood, create the Excitement Factor for another product or task. Then celebrate!

The Excitement Factor can make the difference between a good company and a great company. It has for Oracle. An early Oracle employee once explained his connection with the company to me this way. "There is something that happens about the culture here that I have not experienced at any other company. In your life there will always be that one woman that you love—I realized that Oracle is that company for me. When I came to Oracle to be part of the company early on, I came to help build the company and to be involved with something that is important. When I left Oracle I realized what a fantastic opportunity I had passed up, what a great bunch of people I had worked with, and how much I valued working with blue-chip players. The company is responsive, like Larry's Ferrari." I'd say this employee definitely experienced the Excitement Factor at Oracle!

CHAPTER THREE

Corporate Strategy

EVEN WHEN ORACLE WAS SMALL, THE COMPANY THOUGHT BIG. The prospect of a tiny software startup providing technology that would manage information for all of the corporate world is a tall strategic order, but that was precisely Oracle's vision. And Oracle achieved it, supplying leading-edge relational database technology, tools, and applications to enterprise customers. From there, the aspirations have only grown.

Today, Larry Ellison talks about moving from the Fortune 2000 companies that Oracle currently serves, to the "Consumer Six Billion." By that, he means providing technology and products that can be sold to any consumer. Oracle's next initiative is to provide technology and products that will enable consumer access to electronic information. In an effort to achieve this, Oracle has gone as far as considering buying other large technology companies such as Apple Computer. The company has also considered buying Pacific Gas & Electric's network of wires and cables that connect nearly every home in California, in order to offer products and information to any consumer in the state. These are pretty lofty goals for a company that didn't exist twenty years ago.

Making the company appear larger than it is gives customers and employees a direction; it creates a desire to be part of something that is growing. More importantly, though, setting a lofty goal provides something of a survival mechanism for Oracle. Everyone in the company understands that if Oracle doesn't deliver compelling products and vision to the market, some other company, possibly one based in Redmond, Washington, will.

Oracle holds a number of corporate strategy tenets that are unique to a company of its size. Intended or accidental, each has contributed to the success that Oracle enjoys today:

Eat Your Own Dog Food (Use Your Own Products)

One afternoon, I heard through the rumor mill that an Oracle product manager had presented a new product to Larry Ellison. Apparently the demonstration did not go well, largely because the product manager couldn't use the product. The product manager was fired the next day. The message to the rest of the company was clear: Oracle wants its employees not only to know about Oracle products, but also how to use them!

While this seems like a perfectly reasonable expectation, it's easy for employees to get so caught up in the day-to-day operational details that they forget to put their hands on the product. Oracle tries to avoid this phenomenon by promoting the use of Oracle software by its employees, both inside and outside of the office.

Implement Systems Using Your Software

Oracle, like many companies, maintains a number of large corporate databases. The company is in the unique position of being able to use its own software to run those databases.

The kind of information that Oracle uses its own products to manage includes:

- Customer information
- Helpdesk and support call tracking
- Inventory and order requests
- Payroll and employee data
- Defect tracking system
- Finance and accounting
- Sales force automation

Oracle uses its own products to implement all of these different systems. This way, employees know how to use the products and developers can see their own products "at work" without leaving the campus. The experience is a good one, providing a high level of confidence to the salespeople that Oracle products work and perform the necessary business functions. And it isn't only the developers that Oracle involves in developing and implementing Oracle products to run its business. As early as 1984, Larry Ellison told the CFO, "We're going to run the accounting system on Oracle, and you're going to build it." After recovering from the initial shock that he'd have to build a database application, the CFO began specifying what he needed from an accounting system, then hired developers to create it.

Teach Oracle classes

"You never really know something until you teach it." That is what my mentor told me when I started teaching sailing classes twenty years ago. He was right, and it applies as well to fine-tuning a relational database as it does to keeping a dinghy upright. Oracle product managers and developers often get called to teach a class or to present their product to a user group. The process is educational because the preparation forces a product manager to think about how he or she wants others to understand the product. The actual presentation is also helpful because the product manager knows whether the product and presentation made sense. Of course, both pupils and instructors benefit from the questions and answers provided.

Give your employees an opportunity to become experts in your products

Oracle has set aside labs for employees to configure, test, and use Oracle products. During the time I was responsible for Oracle's desktop network products, I used these labs extensively, spending late evenings fiddling with cables, configurations, and network interfaces so that I would know what it took to use Oracle in a particular network. While some of the time was spent setting up products that were not created by Oracle (for competitive intelligence), the experience was extremely useful when it came time to document a configuration, explain it to a customer, or set it up for a trade show.

Send people to trade shows

There is nothing like putting an employee in the line of fire to give him or her incentive to learn a product. Product managers, developers, and technical writers alike are recruited to go to trade shows—not as spectators—to staff the Oracle demonstration stations. In the Oracle booth, each person is responsible for giving live demonstrations and answering customer questions in front of an audience. Trade shows force employees to prepare a demonstration and learn about products before they get in front of an audience.

Setup competitive products

Oracle has a budget for each department to purchase, install, run, and learn its competitors' products. Both product managers and developers are responsible for knowing whether a competitor's product handles a particular function, and if so, how. The process of setting up a competitor's product can be illuminating in a number of ways. It provides:

- Ideas for how to improve your own product
- Fodder for how to sell against a competitive product
- An understanding of what your customers are seeing in the market
- A chance to think like a customer

Put regular employees on customer support

Oracle customer support is a tremendous machine. This organization, now made up of more than 1,000 people, takes hundreds of thousands of calls every year, assisting customers with everything from installation to system tuning. The customer support operation runs its call tracking system on an Oracle database and accesses the Oracle customer list, which also resides on an Oracle database. Customer support hosts employees from all over the company, including sales, development, marketing, and operations staff who work in customer support for a week at a time answering calls and learning about products.

Be a zealot

In 1992, Oracle produced its first annual report on CD-ROM. It was the first mainstream corporate annual report ever produced on CD-ROM, and Oracle had created the user interface for the CD-ROM using its own multimedia-authoring tool, Oracle Media Objects.

Oracle has even taken the fundamental concept that a company should use its own products and extended it to its customers. For example, when Kellogg's came to visit, the corporate visit center made sure the customer was provided with Kellogg's products for breakfast. At a meeting, the Kellogg's CEO told the Oracle staff that he enjoyed having Kellogg's products, and made it a point to pour an Oracle presenter a bowl of a new cereal so that she could try it.

Training the company to use its own products is not just a great product exercise, it can be a fantastic sales tool. For example, Oracle's CFO now talks with customers about Oracle financial applications, while the head of support joins sales calls where Oracle is selling a helpdesk support application. And of course, Oracle sales representatives are selling the same sales force automation system that they use every day. Any company, in any industry, can gain experience and pride in their products by using what they make.

Build Brand One Word at a Time

Oracle was not always called Oracle Corporation. In the beginning when the company was spending all of its time doing consulting work, it was named Software Development Laboratories. But once Larry and his team decided on the "System R" specification for relational database management, they changed the name of the company to Relational Software Incorporated.

Realizing that it would be difficult to make Relational Software Incorporated a household name, the team chose Oracle as the third name for the company—a name that could specifically be the same as the product name. That way, Larry figured, they could leverage the time and effort spent on developing name recognition.

Over the years, Oracle has spent a lot of time building brand recognition for the Oracle name. Today, Oracle is still the company name and the database name, and all of the complementary products, such as Oracle Forms and Oracle Applications, include "Oracle" in the name. The head of the Network Products group observed, "Larry was very astute to be sure that no product ever eclipsed the greater company."

Contrast this with a smaller software provider in the enterprise area, Blythe Software, which offered a successful front-end tool called Omnis. Blythe became known exclusively for the Omnis product, which became so synonymous with the company that customers referred to the company as Omnis. The company recently capitulated and renamed itself Omnis Software. While this tactic of giving the company and its products the same name is not new—consider consumer products Coca-Cola and Clorox—Oracle was one of the first to bring it to high technology.

In today's crowded market spaces, with thousands of new entrants each year, it's difficult to communicate either a company name or a product name. Oracle quickly realized that trying to communicate the combination of a company name and a different product name would dilute the recognition of both. It chose just one.

Grow Without Acquisition—The Oracle Way

In today's business climate, there is an incredible appetite for acquisition. Companies not growing fast enough on their own look to buy growth, new markets, and new products by acquiring or merging with other companies, even competitors. The predisposition to this activity tells us that it must be successful in some environments. In Oracle's case, however, the greatest part of winning is doing it on its own. A senior Oracle developer explains, "It always takes longer to develop technology internally, but once it's done, you know that it will be a good fit for the product line and it costs less than buying it from the outside."

Early on, Oracle experimented with a technology acquisition, purchasing a product it named Oracle SQL★Calc. The acquired product allowed a user to get data from an Oracle database through an interface similar to a spreadsheet. The technology seemed like a natural extension to the Oracle product offering, and it even came with a small user base. But SQL★Calc was not built the way that other Oracle products were built, and as a result, it was hard for Oracle developers to maintain and enhance the product. "It was not a good thing to be buying technology and trying to smash it in," a developer who worked on the SQL★Calc product told me. The product never truly became integrated into the Oracle product line and gradually faded away.

Earlier, I mentioned that Oracle investigated buying Apple Computer and even looked into buying some right-of-way from Pacific Gas & Electric. Neither of these acquisitions ever took hold, and there were many others along the way that were passed up as well. Most of the few Oracle acquisitions that have been made over the past twenty years have revolved around Oracle buying field consulting or industry experience, not technology.

Although it didn't involve Oracle, a very well-publicized example of a difficult technology acquisition in the database area was Sybase's acquisition of Gain in 1992. Sybase had traditionally lagged behind in the area of application tools technology, and a little company named Gain came to Sybase with a beautiful demonstration of a highly graphical and easy to use tool. Sybase was smitten and jumped to acquire the company, its product, and its people at the rumored price of roughly $70 million. The price was even more surprising to insiders who knew that Gain had minimal revenues and that the technology was not yet in production. Aside from the money it spent on the company, Sybase devoted untold resources to figuring out how to make something useful out of the Gain technology. After several unsuccessful attempts to bring the technology to market, Sybase abandoned the technology and moved on.

More recently, Informix labored heavily from the Illustra acquisition. A small company located in Emeryville, California, Illustra was pioneering a new architecture for databases using object-oriented technology. The product worked in a radically different way from Informix's existing database product, yet Informix tried to offer the Illustra product as Informix's next major release. Customers were not ready to move to the new object-oriented paradigm, and Informix was not ready to offer a new product based on its traditional architecture. As Informix struggled to compete with Oracle, this acquisition put additional strain on Informix.

These examples in mind, Larry Ellison has been very resistant to acquire new technologies, products, or companies. In Oracle's history it has acquired fewer than fifteen technology companies, none of any significant size. This choice to make-versus-buy has helped Oracle steer clear of many of the acquisition disasters that its competition has faced.

Acquiring and successfully integrating that acquired technology is difficult, but Oracle has proven that it is possible to be successful without major technology acquisitions. Any company looking to join forces with another company—whether it's a partner or a competitor—must be completely convinced that the combination of the two will be much greater than the sum of the two individually. The implementation details of integrating new technology, new people, and new products are often larger than they seem.

Locate Your International Headquarters Internationally

Larry Ellison was not a well-traveled man before he founded Oracle. He did not possess the wanderlust that some people have to see the world. Nonetheless, Oracle pressed hard into international markets very early in the development of the company. Oracle's first international presence was a small European distributor named Tom Peddersen Associates that offered Oracle software in Europe as early as 1984. Aside from getting a foothold in the European market, the decision to take Oracle international had an immediate positive impact on the company. Oracle's CFO recalls, "Those guys carried the team for awhile by selling product that was unstable and bringing money in when Oracle really needed it." As soon as Oracle was financially solvent, the company bought out Tom Peddersen Associates, converting all of its employees to Oracle employees.

Based on its success with Tom Peddersen Associates, Oracle soon began offering software through a distributor,

CACI, in London. When Oracle later bought out CACI, it used CACI employees and its location to create Oracle's international headquarters in London, and named a CACI employee to head Oracle International.

Oracle succeeded internationally by starting out with distributors in geographic areas. Even though distributors received good commissions, the cost was worth it because they offered immediate and efficient local support and a local sales presence without the more expensive overhead associated with opening a satellite office or starting a subsidiary. Further, distributors were often also consultants, so they already had expertise in the service side of the business, something that Oracle products need to successfully deliver a complete solution to a customer.

At the time that Oracle was filling out the international organization, running international operations from outside of headquarters was an unconventional strategy for a high-tech company. For Oracle, it proved to be a critical success factor in propelling the company into a global organization, able to serve customers at their convenience in their own countries.

Account for time differences

Although it seems like a simple thing, setting up its international headquarters in the United Kingdom, rather than in California, made Oracle more accessible to Europe and the rest of the world. For the first time, customers in Europe could now call Oracle during its normal business hours and get a live person on the phone. If the need presented itself, a customer could even get a senior manager on the phone and decisions could be made without a day's lag time.

Appreciate language variances

It has been said that America and England are "two countries separated by a common language." To make American marketing literature acceptable in England, words like personalize have to be "Anglicized" to personalise, and the pieces have to be reformatted to fit European-size paper. Because the people responsible for Oracle International had to go through this exercise in order to get their own marketing materials, they were prepared to do the same for distributors in other countries, including those in countries that didn't speak English.

Assist distributors' sales forces

Oracle quickly discovered that international distributors sold a wide range of different hardware and software products, so their sales forces didn't have the time that an Oracle employee had to understand the intricacies of Oracle products. Therefore, field salespeople at distributors had a very different set of needs than Oracle's U.S. field salespeople in terms of materials, training, and support. Fortunately, the international team had been in the same spot just a couple of years before and were able to prepare training and materials that distilled the important points for new distributors. They also quickly provided them with enough information to sell Oracle products within the time limits available to distributor sales forces.

Adapt to international customers' needs

International customers also have different needs than customers based in the United States. On a technical level, they need software that is localized for their particular country. This not only means translation, but also support for completely different character sets. Oracle International set up a localization center and demanded that the core technology group provide basic product enhancements to support software localization. The biggest issue is "multibyte character support" for Asian character sets with thousands of characters. Oracle's core development team then separated out all the message files from the software. Message files contain all the text that a user of the software sees on the screen. This made it easy for Oracle International to translate the database software without the help of the core development team. Additionally, Oracle International understood the logistics of doing business abroad and was better equipped to handle tariffs, duties, and import restrictions locally than from the United States.

Be First in a New Market and Dominate It

With these tenets, Oracle International flourished, so much so that it now represents more than half of Oracle's business. As an Oracle International salesperson explained, "All those sales that Oracle made internationally are sales that a competitor didn't get." And Oracle's advantage was tremendous because none of the other three database providers offered a global solution, enabling Oracle to pursue the largest deals—the ones where large multinationals standardized on the product—with the compelling proposition of local support that the competition couldn't offer.

After positive experiences with Tom Peddersen Associates and CACI, Oracle proceeded to recruit distributors from around the world. In most areas, Oracle got there first and had the only database software presence for many years. This proved to be a great way to gain market share without having to fight with Informix, Ingres, and Sybase.

Oracle International had to accommodate local considerations in every geography. For example, Oracle was prevented from entering the former Soviet Union because as recently as 1992 its software was considered by the U.S. government to contain logic so sophisticated that it could not be exported to countries not friendly with the United States. Russia fell into that category. But in 1993, when the Russian political climate changed, the U.S. government lifted the export restriction on Oracle software. Oracle International scrambled to attack the Russian market, knowing that it would quickly be challenged by competitors, Sybase and Informix, both of whom had made strides in gaining international market share. Within weeks of the export restriction being lifted, Oracle held a seminar in Moscow. Much to the company's surprise, several hundred Russians who currently used Oracle products turned up. Apparently, Oracle software had been as hot on the black market as it was in the hands of the Oracle sales force!

Around 1995, as Oracle continued to grow, the company wanted complete control of its distributors, so it began to convert them to subsidiaries guaranteeing that they would devote 100 percent of their time and effort to selling Oracle. The five useful tactics to be discovered in Oracle's international success can be applied to any business looking to expand into new markets:

1. Be the first into a new market to establish an early easy lead while there is no competition.
2. Leverage the power of distributors if you don't have the resources to hire local staff.

3. Support your distributors well, knowing that you are competing with other product offerings for attention.
4. Create a local office.
5. Locate international headquarters internationally, so as to stay in touch with the issues of an international organization.

Balance Development and Sales

While Larry Ellison maintains a high-profile, visionary outlook outside of the company, his influence inside the company was tempered by the rational voice of Bob Miner. A cofounder, Bob maintained a position as the head of development during the company's formative years. He and Larry could not have been more different in their approaches. While Ellison represented, if not epitomized, an organization of Armani-clad sales professionals who sought only more revenue, Bob stood for structure and rigor. Even when the sales organization continued to demand more products and an endless string of feature requests that would give them more reasons to extract money from a customer, Bob and his team of extremely bright developers stayed the course. But this balance wasn't always easy to maintain.

Individual developers, especially when approached by the head of the company or by a salesperson with a million dollar order on the line, found it difficult to say no to new features. But by the authority of Bob Miner, Oracle engineers were able to say no. A veteran Oracle developer explained to me that, "Early on, Bob Miner had the power to say no and used it. He kept the company focused on the database and the front-end tools. At the time, the company's development process could easily have spun out of control, but he kept focus by saying no."

And spun out of control it well might have since Larry was constantly seeing alluring new opportunities and new product areas—the next golden goose. For example, in the late 1980s, object-oriented technology began to emerge as fashionable. Object-oriented technology allows programmers to build complex software products by reusing small, self-contained, and modular software components called objects. The intrigue of it captivated many within Oracle, but Bob Miner focused his development team on advancing Oracle's core technology. A developer who worked closely with Bob reflected that Bob often said, "No matter what we do here, we cannot go any faster, we cannot put any more people on it, we cannot implement any more features: We are stopping this and we are going to get the product out."

Establishing a strong head of development from the beginning put a hard barrier between sales and development at Oracle. That barrier was a key factor in Oracle's ability to deliver seven major releases of its core database technology in fewer than twenty years. Although Larry continued to be the sales driver, Bob Miner maintained sanity in the development and product release processes. Several developers described the relationship as similar to the U.S. government with its multiple branches of checks and balances, and a long time Oracle executive commented, "The power punch of a high-tech startup is to have a strong technical leader with enough power in the company to stop a powerful sales organization when it has gone overboard, while letting it run as far as it can so that it can work customers and the press."

Managing balance within an organization takes at least two specific, powerful individuals. If one person alone tries to maintain the balance, he or she would have to appear two-faced, taking one position with sales and a different one with development. Having two powerful leaders, one espousing a strong technical vision and another pointing to brilliant sales opportunities, brings both balance and passion to an organization. The lesson to learn from Oracle is not to let an organization get imbalanced, because a sales-centric company will fall short on delivery, while a technology-centric organization will be destined to be destitute.

Foster Entrepreneurship Within

There is a bright and creative entrepreneurial executive who leads a charmed existence at Oracle. Over the years, he has gained the trust of Larry Ellison because he has been able to identify a number of areas where Oracle could benefit by creating a new product. Then, he successfully communicates this market need to the company's president. In many cases, Larry has shared his vision and set him up with a team and a budget and given them room to run.

The first of these entrepreneurial exercises began in 1989 when he went to Larry with the idea of running Oracle software—among the most technically complex, industrial-strength piece of commercial software available at the time—on the Apple Macintosh, then the easiest computer to use on the market. At first glance, it seemed an unnatural combination. The Mac was all about simplicity, while the Oracle database offered the sophisticated developer "as many controls as you find in the cockpit of a 747." This did not deter the individual, whose plan was to make a special version of the database with virtually all of the controls hidden and with a very simple user interface that would be consistent with that of the Macintosh. Larry bought the vision, and the Macintosh group was started up.

The Macintosh team never got very large, operating more like a startup than a group within a large organization, but it executed on a vision: to develop an Oracle product that was easy to use. The team succeeded and, upon completing the product, built packaging that looked different from all other Oracle packaging, packaging that was appropriate for a Macintosh user. The group even set price points that were radically different from the rest of Oracle. At a time when Oracle for DEC VAX was selling for hundreds of thousands of dollars, Oracle for Macintosh was available for $999. It's not important that Oracle didn't sell millions of copies of Oracle for Macintosh, what is important is that the product got Oracle into some very lucrative deals that the competition could not touch because they didn't offer a Macintosh product. Perhaps most importantly though, Oracle for Macintosh demonstrated that Oracle as a company was devoted to every computing platform and that Oracle could build a product that was easy to use.

The launch of Oracle for Macintosh meant the product was now a mainstream Oracle product offering. Thus, the team that developed it moved from its elite entrepreneurship status into a mature business unit, a peer to all of the others in the product porting organization. The transition complete, the executive looked to the next opportunity.

In 1992, Microsoft's Access product, a personal database built to run on Microsoft Windows, caught the attention of low-end database users because of its ease of use and its integration with the Windows operating system. When he discovered that Oracle had nothing to compete with it, he went to Larry. The "Project X" team was immediately formed to build an Oracle product that would run well on

Microsoft Windows and that would provide customers with a better alternative to Microsoft Access. Once again, a small band of entrepreneurial developers worked outside of the normal processes, outside of Bob Miner's development organization and outside of the constraints of Oracle's infrastructure, to develop a new product.

More recently, this executive has participated in many of the new technology initiatives within Oracle. He has been involved with the interactive television project, the network computer team, and, most recently, the Internet database initiative, Oracle 8i. Every one of these entrepreneurial efforts has had a positive impact on the company:

- Generating new products for the company to sell
- Driving product enhancements in other areas of the company
- Creating the public perception of innovation

Although a large organization now, Oracle is still the kind of company that embraces new product ideas and provides an environment to foster their growth. This type of creative thinking provides the following benefits to companies of all sizes.

Creates new products

Common sense tells you that some products developed using this approach make it to market and some do not. Whether they succeed or fail, however, this method is an outlet for getting access to new products. In some ways, the approach of fostering an entrepreneurial environment inside of a company is a substitute for technology acquisition—something that Oracle generally does not do. Instead of acquiring the headaches of personnel or extraneous product integration, organizations can use this method to create and incorporate new products, thereby opening up new opportunities within.

Inspires employees

Oracle values employees with great inner drive and creativity. In Silicon Valley and just about anywhere, it is difficult to attract and keep top talent if employees believe that they will be stifled by the large, traditional organizational mentality. They would rather go to work at a startup company. Despite Oracle's size, employees want to stay because it fosters an entrepreneurial environment where people are excited to work.

Maintains focus

At Oracle, entrepreneurial teams are given space, budget, access to technology, and independence. That's because the company, which has a strong and growing business with its core database product, cannot afford to be distracted by new technologies and "hot" products under development. Keeping new product development separate from its core team affords Oracle the best of both worlds and keeps the size and cost down of new product development teams.

Businesses considering new product or technology areas can benefit from innovation internally and the Oracle formula, which is:

1. Employ leaders who are open to new product ideas or proposals. Although Larry Ellison certainly has his own vision for Oracle, he is open and willing to discuss new product ideas that might enhance Oracle's product offerings.

2. Find a person who already knows the company culture and doctrine and is accepted as an "insider". If you don't, you risk that an entrepreneurial project, even if it is successful, will always be considered an outsider effort and may not be fully accepted by the company at large.

3. Make sure that new ideas are complementary with existing product offerings. Oracle's effort to develop a new architecture for personal computing, the Network Computer, was completely consistent with the company's vision to serve the "Consumer Six Billion." Yet, the Network Computer didn't exactly fit into Oracle's existing product offering, so the company was spun out into a separate organization.

4. Give the idea (and its team) the independence to succeed or fail on its own. Although most were skeptical, Oracle for Macintosh proved to be a successful product, bringing additional deals and a great amount of pride to the team that worked on the project. Without giving its team the independence to try, Oracle probably would not have attempted to develop a Macintosh product.

Drive Productivity with Competition, Not Chaos

In 1989, Larry Ellison decided that he did not want Oracle to be a $500 million company, instead he wanted Oracle to be composed of ten $50 million companies. As a result, Oracle created SBUs (Strategic Business Units), based on product platforms (e.g., IBM, Hewlett-Packard, Digital) to handle different product lines. As a result of this strategy, he developed an environment that fostered internal competition. The product lines had to compete with each other to have the best implementation of Oracle. Additionally, the product lines had to compete with each other for mind share within the Oracle sales force—and money and attention within the company.

Often, Oracle sales representatives encountered a situation where their prospect did not own the hardware on which they were planning to run Oracle software. When customers needed someone to help them decide whether to buy a computer from IBM, Hewlett-Packard, or Digital Equipment Corporation, the Oracle sales representative—perceived as an informed, neutral third party—was called upon to recommend a platform. The Oracle sales representative's decision was usually based on his or her assessment of which computer platform was best able to run Oracle's software. The Oracle sales representative's decision, therefore, represented a sale for one business unit and a lost opportunity for another. As a result, the product lines competed fiercely to build the best Oracle implementation on their particular platform.

Oracle's head of network products told me, "Oracle created people who were religious zealots about each platform. They amplified the best of each platform, even created documentation that was specific to a platform, and they did it all without creating chaos." In many ways, the competition within Oracle drove Oracle to advance its own technology and the platform implementations faster than any external competitor or customer could have.

For example, in 1991, when Oracle was getting ready to launch a new set of tools products called the Cooperative Development Environment, the people organizing the launch set up one room in the executive briefing center with a row of long tables and a different manufacturer's workstation on every table. There were at least eight different computers in the room. They then brought in the product groups to build a demonstration that they wanted Larry to use when he was on stage. Knowing that only two or three of the platforms/demonstrations would actually be used by Larry in his demonstration, each group put additional effort into its software. And because all of the machines were together in the same room, all the groups had an opportunity to see the demonstration that the other groups had done. Each group had to outdo the last so that Larry would choose its work and its platform on which to give the demonstration. The result was a fantastic launch, with each platform team developing excellent demonstration applications that were used for a long time after the launch because they were so good and so complete.

For Oracle, internal competition resulted in superior output. The spirit of internal competition was driven from the top down. A senior marketing person at Oracle recalled, "We would be in meetings and Larry would give the same task to two or three different people, quite openly. That way, those people would have to compete for Larry's attention and would really kill themselves to outperform the others who were doing the same thing."

In the innovative, competitive field of high technology, the strategy of setting up internal competition can be very beneficial from a product development and sales perspective. It relies on employees' creativity and expects them to think out of the box to solve problems and gain new markets. At Oracle, the strategy also fostered a break from some formalized company procedures, but it still followed a rational process, meaning each product group, no matter how creative it was, was still responsible for the basics, such as sales materials, based on the Oracle "look and feel."

While extremely successful for sales and marketing, setting up internal competition may not always be the best strategy from a fiscal perspective. Oracle discovered the downside of internal competition when the organization grew. Many functions were redundant, and the company did not benefit from its scale. "One of the reasons that Oracle went down fast in 1990 was that there were a lot of people—there was a lot of duplication," a senior marketing person told me. Oracle had to consolidate.

One thing that I learned from my Oracle experience is that in a high-growth area, the organization moves fastest with internal competition. Having several employees doing the same thing guarantees urgency. But organizations must create internal competition with the understanding that once the business matures the organization needs to be streamlined, and many employees who were working in parallel on the same objective must be reassigned.

Make Your Enemies' Enemy Your Friend

The concept of aligning against a common evil has been applied to all sorts of relationships over time. After a long history of wars and hatred, the English and the French were able to fight shoulder to shoulder in World Wars I and II because both were threatened by a common enemy. Issues of culture and heritage dropped aside in the face of the German crisis, and these two countries found common ground.

Oracle realized a long time ago that its real enemy was not another relational database vendor. In the long term, Oracle's enemy would not be Sybase or Informix. Its enemy would be Microsoft! As Microsoft pushes into all areas of technology, Oracle's position as a leading supplier of information management products to corporations is clearly in Microsoft's path. In the early days, Oracle knew it would have to beat the other database vendors, but Oracle also knew that it could do that on its own. When it came time for the real war, Oracle would need some big friends.

As early as 1989, Oracle forged a relationship with Apple Computer Inc. A large-scale database manufacturer and a personal computer maker, why did the two bother to collaborate? The answer is the threat of a common enemy, Microsoft. The early collaboration between the two companies led to a series of products that gave Apple's Macintosh platform the ability to access information in an Oracle database and rise to rumors of an Oracle buyout of the computer manufacturer to strengthen its existing position in the market.

More recently, Oracle teamed up with Netscape Communications, Sun Microsystems, and IBM. Support for the Java programming language across all four vendors is one of the results of the union, as is support for the concept of a network computer. Again, the common interest for all is finding a way to unlock Microsoft's stranglehold on the desktop computer.

Finding enemies and forming alliances against them is an easy concept to apply to any business in any industry. Target your company's number one enemy and then figure out what other companies and organizations also have a reason to identify them as an enemy. The strength of the bond between two or more companies that share a common competitor is second only to the strength of a bond between two or more companies that are making money together.

CHAPTER FOUR

Product Development

ORACLE'S PRODUCT DEVELOPMENT STRATEGY HAS UNIQUE ELEMENTS FROM START TO FINISH. Only as an Oracle employee did I begin to understand how the company created an unfair advantage in the marketplace. Unfair, because Oracle doesn't build a product with the hope that customers might be interested in it. Oracle builds a product because a customer or a set of customers requests it. From the beginning, Oracle was founded to fulfill a specific need for a committed customer, originally the Air Force, not to build a speculative product. And using customers as a foundation for a product development strategy makes good business sense, in any industry.

As Oracle grew, the company had the insight to design the database in such a way that it could transcend the computer platform, making the choice of a computer vendor a commodity detail, and making the choice of a database vendor a key strategic decision. The company also had the wisdom to permeate information throughout its organization so it could execute cleanly on its vision of complete Oracle portability. The philosophy behind Oracle product development isn't a secret. In fact, it is Oracle's ability to execute many of the fundamentals better than other companies that makes the company so successful in managing products, processes, developers, and communications.

Develop for the "Built-in Consumer"

Oracle is successful because Larry Ellison understood the fears of system administrators throughout the world. He considered the questions that kept them up at night. Will I choose the right computer hardware? Will I choose the right operating system? Will I choose the right network? Will I lose my job? Then, Larry carefully set the Oracle vision to assuage their fears.

Oracle promised to run its software on any hardware, network, and operating system, so a nervous information systems manager never had to worry if he or she chose an Oracle database. In fact, Oracle ran several advertisements saying "No One Ever Got Fired for Choosing Oracle." Often, these ads featured a timid looking IS executive or a jumble of computers, wires, and different software boxes. To make good on the vision, Larry tasked the development organization to make the Oracle database universal. That way, Oracle could run on every available brand of server in the world, from huge mainframes to personal computers. It could also run on every different type of network in the world and people could access information using any computer including a PC, a Macintosh, and a Unix workstation.

From the beginning, the Oracle product philosophy has been organic and included the "built-in customer" concept. No product is built without a specific customer or set of customers who request it. Then, fundamental questions must be satisfactorily answered before development work starts on a product. These questions include:

- Who is demanding the product?
- What are they willing to pay for the product?
- How long will they use it?

- What are they going to use it for?
- Can this product be sold to other businesses?

Oracle has been able to rely on its built-in consumer strategy because it caters to customers in a number of ways. Architects from the core technology team are often called into a high-profile customer site to investigate a problem that technical support cannot solve. While there, developers get to see, in person, how the limits of the database are pressed in a real industrial-strength environment. They also get to talk to the people who are on the front line of information management. I believe that many of the feature enhancements for new Oracle database releases come from conversations with customers.

Clearly, the size, stature, and potential of a particular customer at Oracle also dictates the impact that customer can have on a product. Some customers do not make any impact on a product, while others are large enough to merit a product of their own.

While I was at Oracle, the investment banking firm of Goldman Sachs was one of the customers that rose to the top in terms of size, stature, and potential. The firm had very specific objectives regarding what it wanted to do with Oracle technology. Members of its technical team met with Oracle employees in New York and at Oracle headquarters in California to explain the changes that Goldman wanted in Oracle's front-end tool, SQL★Forms. Not only was what the firm wanted something that Oracle did not have, it was something that Oracle did not plan to support. To satisfy Goldman Sachs, however, Oracle created a special version of SQL★Forms specifically for the firm. One of the SQL★Forms developers told me, "I would go through the code for the SQL*Forms and see logic that was marked for Goldman Sachs only!" When Oracle released the standard version of SQL*Forms, development also released a special version just for Goldman Sachs.

The interaction that Oracle promotes between customers and developers has resulted in Oracle delivering very few unsuccessful products to market. It has also promoted a responsive product development process that has seen back-to-back success of Oracle's Versions 5, 6, 7, and 8 database releases. Each product met the market needs for its time and consistently received favorable press coverage and customer acceptance upon its release.

Make Your Product Strategic to the Customer

One of Oracle's greatest product development strengths was, and continues to be, its ability not to accept the status quo. When Oracle saw a chance to reset the rules of the industry, to make other companies dependent on Oracle for their success, Oracle took the chance. And it paid off.

In the 1980s, there were very few standards for computers. Each vendor built its own hardware that was different from every other vendor's hardware. Further, each vendor built system and application software that could only run on its hardware. For anyone with big computing needs, choosing a computer manufacturer was a strategic decision that could result in a huge success or a waste of millions of dollars. During this period, software developers also had to make choices. They had to bet that a particular computer manufacturer (e.g., IBM, Hewlett-Packard, Digital, NeXT) would be successful when they chose to build their software for that platform. If a software developer was correct about the computer platform the company chose, that developer had a chance to do well. If the developer was wrong, the company would almost certainly suffer.

Larry Ellison and his company set out to solve the technical problems associated with running Oracle software on any computer. If Oracle could accomplish this, Oracle could make the choice of computer platform irrelevant. In the process, Larry and his team were able to deliver peace of mind to customers and establish a real competitive advantage for Oracle. Thus, Oracle invented the concept of porting for commercial database products. Porting is the process of adapting a software application so that it can run on a range of computers from different manufacturers.

At the time, porting was not only unusual, it was extremely difficult. First, many of the computers used different programming languages. To adapt software from one language to another required a complete rewrite of the basic software application. Oracle's first task was to find a language that would be common to the assortment of computers available at the time. The leading contender was a language called C, which was developed in the university community to be portable so programs written in it could run on many different computers. While C was not available on all of the platforms of the day, it was available on some platforms and showed promise for the future.

Next, Oracle had to recreate the Oracle database using the C language. This involved rewriting Version 3 (the next version) of Oracle in the new language. But while working on this task, Oracle's core team developers discovered that the language was not completely portable. Different hardware vendors had added things to the university specification of the C language that ran on their computers to enhance and differentiate their own product offerings. To work around this, Oracle developers learned to use only the pieces of the C language that were common to many different platforms so that their code would be portable. The core team also developed a program called "Olint" in the process that could read all of the code that they had written and pick out things that might make the Oracle database software nonportable.

In order to take advantage of the different offerings that the hardware manufacturers had provided to their computers, Oracle also built a small piece of software called the operating system dependent interface (ODI). This software was designed by an expert who knew about many different computers and operating systems. From then on, all of the details specific to a particular computer were kept in the operating system dependent interface, so when Oracle wanted to port its database to a new computer, all it had to change was that small piece of software.

"The early developers at Oracle really took the C language to its highest level," a senior developer told me. "Oracle was truly a pioneer in this area, using C on platforms where no one else was using C." At a time when university students were playing with the language, Oracle was building a large-scale, industrial-strength application with it. But Oracle's pioneering in this area was not easy. Oracle found it difficult to find C development tools from many of the hardware manufacturers and had to search them out from third parties, including other pioneers in this area, WhiteSmith and Lattice. At one point, Oracle simply could not find a C compiler for a particular platform, so an early Oracle engineer sat down and wrote it himself. The C implementation and its resulting portability is the technology crown jewel of Versions 5 and 6 of the Oracle database.

On an implementation level, once Oracle was able to prove portability, a very significant product development phenomenon occurred. Oracle was able to turn the tables on the computer manufacturers. While once the manufacturers had been able to take advantage of software vendors who had made a commitment to their platform, manufacturers now had to pursue Oracle to port its database software to their computers. This sales effort by the manufacturers resulted in Oracle getting free computers and lots of support so that the Oracle software would run better on their computer hardware than on competitors' hardware. At a time when Oracle needed to reinvest all it could in development and sales, the strategy of porting really helped Oracle's expenses.

Porting brought another significant phenomenon to Oracle's marketing and sales. An Oracle marketing veteran reminds me, "No one ever bought a database because Oracle pioneered the use of C. The use of C is what let Oracle deliver on the dream of portability, and that promise made a market." The ability to move Oracle software quickly to any new or trendy operating system—particularly when a deal called for it—let Oracle in on opportunities that were simply closed to the competition. On the strategic level, the portability strategy was brilliant. "It was one of the most insightful customer perceptions that Oracle ever made," a past head of the Network Product Division told me. In implementation, it was effective because it let an Oracle sales representative walk in to a prospective customer and say, "Don't worry what computer you buy, as long as you buy Oracle."

One of the best examples I encountered about the selling power associated with portability came from a presentation the former head of the Network Product Division was giving to a large customer. The Oracle executive was talking about an Oracle networking product named SQL*Net, and the audience, composed of a number of employees of the customer were nitpicking feature after feature. The customers kept questioning Oracle's implementation of very specific technical features, including two-phase commit and row level locking, and were very negative in general. After about an hour of difficult questions, the Oracle manager stopped and said, "Excuse me, but based on your questions, it sounds to me like Oracle is the only solution that will run on all of your machines. We should be figuring out how to implement Oracle in your shop." After a pause, the customer group glanced around at each other and was cooperative and supportive for the rest of the talk. The power of porting had made Oracle the only choice.

While the market is certainly different today—C is a mainstream computer language and every respectable software company is capable of porting its software to new and different computers—the important idea to take away from Oracle's experience is this: In the beginning, Oracle was beholden to the industry's hardware manufacturers, but the company saw a chance to reset the rules of the industry and took it! Oracle made the required investment to make the computer a commodity so that it could position the Oracle database at the top of the technology food chain. Oracle, then, was in a position of control over the computer manufacturers, sales, and its customers.

Today, it's not difficult to find examples of companies changing the rules in any industry. The key is understanding how to make your offering not a commodity component of a sale, but the key decision factor in a complete strategy and investment.

Build with Failure in Mind

Oracle's product development team fully understands that software sometimes fails. With this in mind, the company has implemented technology to gracefully handle a variety of system errors and failures.

Although there are many factors that can cause an Oracle database to stop functioning, the only factor within an Oracle developer's control is when the Oracle database software stops or crashes. All of the other failure conditions that a database experiences are out of Oracle's control, for example:

- Someone pulling the plug on the computer that is running the database
- Another application running on the computer that crashes and halts the whole computer
- A network failure
- A computer hardware failure, such as a hard disk crash

Nothing in Oracle software can guard against the above failure conditions, and for Oracle's first three versions, these kinds of problems meant possible disaster for a customer's data. Imagine a customer standing at an automated teller machine. There are a number of steps that a customer takes in the simple task of withdrawing money. During the transaction, any failure in the system could cause problems either with the bank's database or the customer's pocketbook.

There are eleven discrete steps associated with taking money out of an ATM (from a database perspective):

1. Customer inserts ATM card
2. Customer enters security code
3. ATM sends message across network to customer database to check security code
4. Database checks security code
5. Database sends message back saying that security code is OK
6. Customer asks to withdraw $100
7. ATM sends a message across the network to the account database
8. Database deducts $100 from the customer's account balance
9. Database sends message back saying that $100 has been deducted
10. Machine spits out five crisp $20 bills
11. Customer signs off ATM (takes card)

What if there was a construction crew digging in the street and exactly at Step 8 it severed the network connection from the ATM to the main database? The customer has $100 deducted from his or her account but has not gotten the actual money. This is exactly the type of problem that Oracle set out to solve with Version 5 of its database. Oracle developers implemented the idea of a "transaction," where every one of the steps of a transaction had to take place for the entire transaction to be valid. The developers built "log files" to store each tiny step of a transaction, so that if the transaction failed somewhere in the middle, the Oracle database could recover gracefully.

In the case of the ATM and the construction crew, the database would never have gotten a message back from the ATM saying that the transaction was complete. The database would have recognized that the transaction had failed when it did not receive a message back from the ATM, so the database would have declared the entire transaction invalid. In that case, the database would have "rolled back" the customer account to its original state before the transaction started and would have left the $100 in the customer's account.

Bob Miner, cofounder and long time head of Oracle development, felt that Oracle had reached maturity with its Version 5 database "when Oracle designed a product knowing that it could fail." Based on the understanding that some failure conditions were simply out of Oracle's control, Oracle implemented technology to elegantly handle all sorts of system errors and failures.

This concept of designing a product with failure in mind is one that the automobile industry has also embraced, although it took them longer than Oracle. While cars are being built to be more reliable everyday, there are some failure conditions that auto makers simply cannot control. One is car crashes. The manufacturers can make cars stop faster and easier to turn so that drivers will have fewer crashes, but there are still accidents. To help handle these error conditions more gracefully, the auto makers designed seat belts, and later, air bags inside of cars. While these improvements came more than fifty years after the invention of the car, they do a great deal to help what the manufacturer cannot prevent.

Anyone involved in the business of making products should be looking at how they could potentially fail, both to figure out how prevent the failure and to figure out how to handle failure in the event that it cannot be prevented.

Whatever You Do—Ship!

Referring to the best lesson he learned during his time at Oracle, a past development head told me, "The best feature a product can ever have is SHIPPING."

This strategy, known to some as the "release early, release often" principle, can be applied to any product company in any market. The fanciest television in the world will not create any revenue or recognition for its manufacturer unless the set is commercially available.

Oracle taught this lesson over and over again. Just look at its product shipping history. Oracle recently released Version 8 of its core database product, marking seven major releases, seven complete new versions of the product to customers, in fewer than twenty years. Given the depth of technical sophistication of an Oracle database—the porting, documentation, testing, and support involved in each release—this is a remarkable accomplishment. To get a feel for the kind of process and change that Oracle faces, imagine the logistics that Ford Motor Company might face if it wanted to completely design and release a brand new model of every car in its line every three years.

After building his first house, a friend of mine told me that you can't build a house right until you do it a second time. With all of the experience that you have gained from the first, you will know how to get exactly what you want, and avoid the pitfalls, with the second.

Likewise, a senior developer at Oracle remarked, "No product is truly successful until Version 3 successfully ships. Oracle did a good job of getting to Version 3 quickly. The faster a company can get to Version 3, the better off it is. Ship as many versions as quickly as possible—get features into customer's hands. A company is better off choosing more frequent releases."

Oracle's continuous product release process has enabled developers at the company to iterate on features and implementations, so that Oracle can have a product that is built right, before the competition has released a product at all.

Focusing on getting new technology into customers' hands in a timely manner is one of the critical success factors that has kept Oracle in front of its competition. While there were times when Oracle was behind a competitor in functionality, it was never a long period. The Oracle "machine" would quickly promise and produce a release to address the competitor's issues, and in the process develop more, even better, features. With every new release, Oracle reset the bar—the criteria on which databases were judged.

"The real differentiator that Oracle had against, for example, IBM—which had researched and developed the relational database in the first place—was that Oracle was able to turn it into a shipping product," noted an early Oracle employee.

The lesson learned: No matter what product you produce, ship it first.

Anticipate the Next Wave

In some ways, Larry Ellison is an oracle. One of the greatest gifts he has given to the company is his ability to see the future. "Larry's world is 18 months ahead of ours," the vice president of desktop development told me in late 1989. At the time, Larry had announced a product upon which work had just begun, and we were running around trying to figure out how we could deliver faster on his announcement.

In Larry's mind, products that are being released today have already been phased out. Products that are on the drawing board today are just being released. And products that no one has even thought of are sketched on the drawing board in his mind.

For example, in 1988, when Larry looked ahead, he realized that after he had sold a database to every business in the world, he would need more products to sell them. The obvious answer was applications: applications that would sit on top of and use Oracle databases to perform functions such as inventory management, personnel recording, and field sales force automation. For example, an employee could use a password-protected personnel database to look up another employee's company phone number or e-mail address, while the human resources manager could use the database to look up payroll or health benefits information. Oracle's applications, because they were completely integrated with the core database product, would make Oracle technology truly "turnkey," meaning that customers could buy a database and an application and get their inventory or personnel system up and running without any development.

The task of building Larry's vision into Oracle applications was assigned to a new hire with a strong industry background. A thick-skinned visionary, this executive progressed toward Oracle's application dream for almost six years. During those years, the Applications Group was under a great deal of fire internally because the team, often considered the black sheep of Oracle, had (on average) more than 100 people but had never released a production product or generated much revenue.

Even though reductions in the applications team were threatened during the Oracle stock crash of 1990, Larry stuck to his dream, finally producing Oracle's database applications. A glance at the Oracle annual report today proves the vision was right on target. In 1997, the company generated nearly $300 million in license revenues of Application products, and an additional $390 million in Applications-related services.

In keeping with Oracle's product development philosophy of releasing products often, the Applications Group has worked steadily to produce release after release. Over the course of the last twelve years, the group has been able to deliver a new major release almost every year and is currently offering Version 11 of some applications.

The important element to take away from this is not to be satisfied with getting your product out the door. That is a tremendous accomplishment, but you have to build the development of future iterations and variations of your product into your development cycle now.

Nurture Your Core Team

In a competitive industry like high technology, many companies would trade five marketing or sales people for one good developer. Today, Oracle has more than 2,000 developers. Of this formidable staff, there is a small team of approximately forty engineers who design and build Oracle's core database software product. Oracle's elite group is known as the "kernel group," and it is truly the heart of Oracle technology. The development that all of the other technical staff at Oracle does is based on the work performed by the kernel group: moving the database to new hardware platforms, building development tools, even creating finished software applications.

Over time, a lot of experience has been built up in the kernel team. Unlike other areas of the company that can afford turnover, and in some cases need turnover to stay fresh, Oracle has managed to maintain stability and experience in the kernel group. Although Oracle tries to satisfy all of its employees, the company makes particular attempts to keep its core developers happy. Some of the tactics designed specifically to keep stability in the core team developers so they can deliver quality year after year include:

Maintain focus

In their combined twenty-five-plus years with Oracle, the kernel team marketing and development managers have managed to consistently drive the course of the group. The mission has always been to advance Oracle's core database technology, and they use their secret mix of customer input, competitive knowledge, and intuition to set that course. They refuse to be distracted by technology fads. This continuity, combined with the knowledge that the group will not have a new manager every six months, gives the whole team a consistent feel, providing stability in both product direction and staff.

Hire well

The leaders of the kernel team always hired slowly to maintain the integrity of the group. The core team leaders understand that the group has to expand, so they hire continually. This gradual influx of people allows managers to develop each individual, grooming them for their prized place at the heart of Oracle.

Develop new hires

At Oracle, there is more emphasis in the kernel group than in any other group to continually grow the number of members so that it can expand as the company and the industry does. In this environment, developing new hires means including them in open strategy discussions about the future of the technology, encouraging them to attend research presentations in various areas, and giving them time to install and use competitive products.

Keep employee consistency from version to version

In any industry, the way an employee learns to build a product right is to build it the first time. The process of building a software product teaches a programmer the pitfalls, so when it is built a second time, it can be built correctly. This applies particularly to the kernel team where employees are encouraged to continually improve the core code, rather than some extension to the product that may or may not be part of an upcoming release. In an environment where the majority of the company is reorganized on an annual basis, many of the staff involved in designing and building the core product have worked on the last five or six major versions. With that kind of consistency, the kernel team brings all of its experience to the next version of Oracle software.

Reward with stock options

The kernel team is famous for being rewarded with new and larger grants of stock options. Anyone who has been in this group through the building of a couple of versions and has held on to these stock awards has amassed a retirement fund that is probably in the seven figures. These rich rewards are the incentives that keeps people in the group.

Maintain high visibility with top management

Larry Ellison, quite wisely, pays a lot of attention to the kernel team. After all, the future of his company is riding on each release. The honor of warranting attention from a CEO has a great impact on keeping people on the core team.

Promote "team mystique"

Because the kernel team is revered from top to bottom as being the heart of Oracle, a mystique has developed around the group. I liken it to being a Navy SEAL. The SEALs are the best of the best, considered elite due to the effort required to get accepted into the group. They are there because they want to be there and were talented enough to get there. The honor that comes with being a part of that team is one of the reasons they keep doing it. The feeling is similar within Oracle's kernel group.

Foster camaraderie

Having a small, cohesive, successful group that works together on a project is self-perpetuating. The members of the kernel team work together, have lunch together and some even go skiing at Lake Tahoe together. The sense of community the team fosters is yet another bonding factor that keeps the kernel team satisfied.

In reference to the kernel team, a former Oracle executive said, "Having the people and their knowledge is worth more than the product itself." With a strong team, a company can always build another product, whereas the strength of a product is only as good as the product's lifetime.

Every company has something special at its center. Perhaps it's the technology, perhaps it's the selling model. Whatever "it" is, the responsibility lies with the company to nurture that special ingredient, to make sure that it is satisfied, so that it grows. Oracle does a number of things to make sure that its kernel team is happy and productive, but each one of them can be translated to assist any company in any industry with the nurturing of its own core team.

Permeate Your Organization with Information

While Oracle promotes mysticism around its core development team, it does not encourage secrecy when it comes to product releases or schedules. In fact, Oracle is committed to flooding the organization with information.

But it was not always that way. During my first month at Oracle, some of the product managers and I met with Oracle's telesales force. In the first of the presentations, one of the product managers discussed the competitive points of his product, as well as upcoming features. Before he could continue, he was met with resounding voices. "We want dates!" chanted his well-dressed, aggressive audience of employees capable of selling $50,000 worth of software over the phone. Quick on his feet, the single presenter brought them to laughter by telling them that he was actually looking for a "date" himself. He was not able to give them the key piece of information they wanted, though. In the early days of any company, the issue of getting product release information to the sales force is no joke. Oracle was not an exception.

Today, the company has changed. Oracle posts an upcoming product delivery schedule, by month, in every hallway. It is not detailed; it simply lists the products by name that will be released during any given month. Out in the open, every Oracle employee looks at these schedules, and as a result every worker—from developers to product managers, from junior assistants to Larry Ellison—has the ship dates of every Oracle product stamped onto his or her brain. Providing this information means every development team takes great pride in getting a "Delivered—On Time" stamp when its product ships, and every salesperson rests more easily knowing that development has promised the same dates they have.

Additionally, Oracle distributes a "Red Packet" to keep all of its employees in touch with customers. The Red Packet is released monthly and it contains any new Oracle marketing materials that have been written in the course of the past month. Often it contains user success stories that give sales, support, and development employees insight into how real people are using their products. A development head told me that he took a morning every month to read through the Red Packet, and that same afternoon he would devote to planning new features for his product.

Providing critical information to employees not only spares product managers from salespeople, chanting and desperate for information, but it keeps the entire organization better informed. Since Oracle began posting the release date schedules, there has been a much higher level of communication about new products.

It works. In 1993 the entire Oracle world was expecting a new release of the Database Forms tool in July. The product managers took a few minutes every day in the weeks before the product launch to send out a quick note to the sales force with some piece of information about the new product. Some days it was a competitive blurb, other days a new feature, but I am convinced that this happened every day because the product manager saw the product release schedule in the hallway on her way into the office in the morning and on her way back from lunch, and she acted because of it.

Communicating within any organization is a critical component of product development because it provides a way for all employees to be kept apprised of product features, benefits, and schedules. Publicized deadlines and features can also motivate employees to meet product goals—and meet them on time!

CHAPTER FIVE

Incredible Selling Power

ARLY IN ORACLE'S HISTORY, THE CHIEF FINAN-
CIAL OFFICER ASKED LARRY ELLISON WHY HE
THOUGHT ORACLE HAD TO GROW SO FAST. "Why don't we
slow down, so we don't make so many mistakes?" Larry's
response: "How much do you think Pepsi has to spend to buy
one-half of one percent of the soda market?" The answer was
obvious. Pepsi, like so many other companies that enter a
market in second place, had to spend a lot of money.

Larry saw Oracle's potential and, like Coke had done
before Pepsi, saw a market opportunity and a chance to cap-
ture market share, brand awareness, and customer loyalty
while it was still affordable to do so. Prior to the entrance of
other competitors, Oracle set a course to push full steam
ahead into a new market in order to own it. And in its brave
new world, Oracle had one distinct advantage over Coke:
Businesses would buy Oracle databases, and when they did
so, they would make a large financial and long-term commitment to the technology company.

Unlike Coke, Oracle also had an external market factor
working to its advantage. As Oracle and some of its early
competitors began to deliver products, the market
demanded that a company—ANY company—take a leadership position and establish a standard. This phenomenon is
common to new product areas where several competitors

come out with competing standards. Buyers, afraid of choosing the "wrong" standard, look for any sign of market dominance so that they can bet on the "right" standard. A good example was the introduction of the video cassette recorder (VCR) in the late 1970s. While Betamax and VHS battled fiercely, VHS was able to establish a slight edge and the market quickly solidified in its direction. Few consumers then risked purchasing a Betamax VCR and the product became obsolete.

Determined to win early market share, Oracle built a sales force with incredible selling power. Its legendary proficiency and the ways Oracle managed that sales force, ranging from aggressive compensation planning to complete infrastructure creation, provide insight into how a company can accelerate growth into a new, better market.

Build Incentives that Get Sales' Attention

The Oracle sales force is extreme in every way. Nothing matters but numbers, and there is no substitute for revenue. Salespersons who make their numbers at Oracle are well compensated, better than most in the industry. Salespeople who don't make their numbers are fired.

The original tenets of the Oracle sales force were instilled by Oracle's early heads of sales. During the 1980s, these executives had a reputation for being tough, hands-on managers who wanted Oracle to win at any cost. In important deals where Oracle encountered competition, they got personally involved. They also made personal visits to customers, slashed prices, and promised future deliverables until those in his path said yes. The legacy remains, and these tactics are still widely employed by Oracle salespersons.

In the early days, compared to IBM or Digital, Oracle had little traditional sales training, yet aspiring sales executives flocked to the startup. The reason was CASH! Oracle provided an incentive that mattered. More than once, Larry Ellison proudly remarked, "My best salesperson makes more than I do." The lore of individual Oracle salespersons making $200,000, $300,000, $500,000 per year is supported by several overachievers who retired after just a few of years in the Oracle sales force.

The key to Oracle's sales incentive is the "accelerator." It dictates that salespersons are entitled to a commission of a certain percentage of the dollar volume they sell within their quota. Sell more than quota and the real money starts to roll in. For example, if a salesperson has a quota of $1,500,000 in revenue per year, that salesperson receives a modest base salary of $30,000 plus a commission of 5 percent on revenue up to the $1,500,000 quota. If that salesperson makes quota, he or she makes $105,000. For revenue generated above quota, the commission "accelerates." For the first $500,000 in revenue generated over quota, the salesperson gets a commission of 6 percent, and for the $500,000 after that the salesperson gets a commission of 8 percent. The next $500,000 gets compensated at 10 percent, and so on up. For example, a salesperson who was able to sell $3 million of Oracle software in a year, the result is:

$30,000	Base Salary
$75,000	Commission on $1,500,000 at 5 percent
$30,000	Commission on the next $500,000 at 6 percent
$40,000	Commission on the next $500,000 at 8 percent

$50,000   Commission on the next $500,000 at
            10 percent

Total income: $225,000

Not bad for a year of selling Oracle database software!
But that's just where it starts, because the accelerators keep
increasing as a percentage of revenue generated. A company
with a direct sales force that wants to grow its revenues may
want to investigate the accelerator model for sales compensation as a way to encourage exactly what the company
wants to achieve.

However, one of the risks that any business with an
aggressive sales force faces is that the company will gain that
kind of a reputation. At the end of the 1980s, at the height
of Oracle's aggressive selling binge, I often heard the following kinds of comments and jokes from both outside and
inside of the organization:

"We not only sell smoke, we deliver it."
"It's not lying, it's positioning."
"We build 'Just-In-Time' software."
and
Q: What is the difference between a used car salesman
   and an Oracle salesman?
A: The used car salesman knows when he is lying!

Whether they were too aggressive or not, Larry Ellison
was behind Oracle's sales force 100 percent. One of
Oracle's earliest finance people told a story that illustrates
Larry's commitment to the sales force. From the very start,
Oracle's finance department made an effort to set policies
and procedures for how Oracle's money was managed. At

the time, as is the case now, there were limits on the quantity and timing of travel advance money. Although the policy was common knowledge, salespeople would come to the finance department a day before a trip needing a large advance. Finance would say no, according to policy. Shortly after the salesperson was sent away, Larry would call down to finance and say: "Salespeople are like gold. Give them whatever they want." This scenario played itself out time after time, but this special treatment was only ever extended to salespeople.

Create Infrastructure that Supports Revenue Generation

Early on, Oracle did a fantastic job of focusing its expensive, high-profile field sales people on big deals, creating a tremendously lucrative, accelerator-based commission plan to provide incentive. At the same time and of equal importance, Oracle created an infrastructure within the company to propel field sales professionals toward the next big deal. Key to Oracle's success was its establishment of specialized profit areas that didn't require the attention of Oracle's seasoned selling experts. These areas, which included support, education, consulting, and services, provided ways for Oracle to stay close to its customers—and continue to generate smaller amounts of money from them—while allowing its field sales force to stay focused on the multimillion dollar deals.

Centralized support

At first, Oracle handled customer support through its field sales offices. Each sales office had a number of field support engineers who were teamed up with salespersons.

This strategy was excellent for staying close to customers when Oracle's technology was young and the company needed customers to serve as reference accounts. This tactic also kept salespersons involved with an account long after the initial sale because support was being handled by a local field support engineer. Thus, problems or questions caught the attention of the salesperson. Being so close to an account gave the Oracle salesperson "depth of vision," meaning he or she knew what the account needed, which enabled the salesperson to go back and sell upgrades or maintenance contracts as the customer deployed more Oracle technology.

As Oracle grew, the pressures of revenue and of organizational scalability forced change in customer support. While maintenance and upgrade contracts were easier to close than initial license sales, the money involved was only a fraction of the size of the original deal. And the vice president of sales decided that he didn't want his selling elite to spend time on these low-dollar value contracts. He wanted his team out slaying the next dragon. So he took control of the customer support function, centralized it at Oracle headquarters, and made it a profit center. From that point forward, any upgrade or maintenance revenue had to go through the support organization. Suddenly, the customer support group was responsible for selling all upgrades and maintenance contracts—turning a previous cost center into a very lucrative profit center for Oracle. Mission accomplished. The field salespeople no longer faced the distraction of relatively small-dollar maintenance contracts—because these contracts were now executed through support—and the field no longer received credit for ongoing support and maintenance revenue. And the organization could scale in a more linear way as Oracle added customers across geographies and industries.

Education and consulting

The effort to focus field sales away from account management and onto new business did not stop with the reorganization of the customer support organization. Oracle also created profit centers to handle education and consulting. Instead of using a field salesperson to provide consulting services to customers rolling out an Oracle database, the field salesperson could turn planning and implementation questions over to one of these organizations, which, in turn, would charge the customer for the service. Again, the field salesperson escaped the details of account management and was free to pursue the next large new opportunity.

Advanced services

Even engineering didn't stop Oracle sales from making that next big deal. One of the problems that Oracle field sales encountered when it went after lucrative deals was that Oracle did not always have all of the products necessary to fulfill a customer's requirements. Often there were interface products missing. For example, in one case an enormous potential customer was still using an old IBM database product called IMS (Information Management System), and the customer was not ready to export all of its information out of IMS into Oracle. The customer also wanted its users to be able to get to information in both its IMS and its new Oracle database, and the deal hinged on Oracle's ability to deliver that functionality. At the time, Oracle did not have a product to connect an Oracle database to an IMS database, and the development group had no intention of building such a product.

For many companies, this would have been the end of the sale, but Oracle smelled opportunity. Development was not going to build the product, so the Oracle sales group created its own development team, called Advanced Services. The Advanced Services group, which has been roughly twenty staff strong since its inception, performs custom development work for large customers. In the case of the customer with the IMS database, Advanced Services built software to make the needed connection. Because this work was being done on a custom basis and the product was not on the price list, the Oracle sales representative could charge as much as he wanted (or could obtain) for the work. The best part was that when Oracle found a second customer with the same need, the company could charge for the work all over again! The Advanced Service team, aside from being another lucrative profit center for the company, enabled a salesperson to enlarge a deal Oracle otherwise would have had to walk away from because it did not have all of the products.

Telesales

In addition to the powerful field sales force that Oracle built, the company also created a hungry telesales team. Initially built to answer the phones that rang as a result of Oracle advertisements, the Oracle telesales force quickly grew in size and selling ability. And the people on the phone began to fight with the people in the field over specific customer opportunities. The clash was almost inevitable, as many of the original telesales people had been Oracle field representatives who were tired of the travel and the rigors of being in a field office and had elected to move into a headquarters job.

Again, Oracle was able to solve two problems with one solution. Problem number one was the contention between the two sales teams, but problem number two was how to focus the more expensive field salespeople on the higher dollar value deals. The solution: Oracle set an arbitrary floor on the deal size that an Oracle field representative could offer to a customer. Initially, the smallest deal a field salesperson could offer was $15,000, but that number quickly grew to $35,000 and today is over $50,000. Although a line was drawn, telesales continued to be aggressive, even figuring out how to split an $80,000 deal into two different purchase orders so the deal could fall into the telesales realm. The fierce competition meant that the only way that a field salesperson was sure to get credit for a particular transaction was to make sure that it was a big one.

Presales

Another mechanism that Oracle used effectively to keep its sales representatives moving from big deal to big deal was presales. The job of the presales group was to provide technical expertise before the sale to the salesperson and the customer to make sure that the customer's expectations were in line with the actual product functionality, and to make sure that the customer was excited about buying Oracle. In this position, presales people walk that delicate line between being technical support and advisor to the customer who is evaluating many products and coach to the salesperson who needs to understand what is going on inside the customer's technical organization. While presales employees were located in the field and assigned to individual salespeople, they functioned like product managers. In fact, some of them ended up being very successful product managers because of their strong understanding of customer issues and requirements.

With profitable support, education, consulting, and services, Oracle's sales team didn't have to worry about ongoing account management. It also wasn't put off by a hole in the product offering and did well if it brought lots of big new deals into the company. Creating a focused sales force takes more than a good compensation plan, it takes an infrastructure that is ready to be responsible for your customer once the initial deal is done.

Go Straight to the Top

While many businesses may not find themselves in a leading market position, any business can learn from the success of the Oracle sales strategy, which is to sell high in the organization and establish a strategic relationship with the customer.

Oracle sales was successful because it was able to identify the "Point of Pressure" in the market, and it built an organization to exploit it. The Point of Pressure for Oracle is the Fortune 500 chief technical officer (CTO). Caught between information overload, user demand, and new technology, the CTO is not an easy person with whom to communicate.

Oracle built a sophisticated sales organization designed to reach that Point of Pressure. Its great compensation plan attracted the high-end sales talent necessary to interact with a stressed-out CTO, and its management philosophy of getting the sale at all costs backed those people up with the support it took to make commitments in sales situations.

In order to continue servicing the CTO population, Oracle has built a worldwide sales and consulting force that is more than 5,000 people today. The commitment to exploiting the Point of Pressure continues naturally into Oracle marketing programs, and even into the development groups who are responsible for regular visits to high-profile customers.

From the very start of Oracle, Larry Ellison has known the importance of selling his products to the most senior executive he could reach. As a result, Larry built a sales force of polished sales professionals who had the image, the intelligence, and the Rolodex to call on senior officers of a large company. Finding and attracting individuals that have these three attributes is not easy, but it has paid off in a number of tangible ways for Oracle.

High average selling price

Oracle software is expensive. Software to support a large company can cost in the millions of dollars. Only senior people in large companies have spending authority for that kind of money and can make decisions on large purchases quickly. Oracle salespeople know how to talk to this level officer about solving business problems, not about nifty technology features. As a result, they are able to execute large transactions more quickly.

Corporate standardization

One of the benefits about selling to a senior person in an operation is that this person has control over one (or many) division(s). Making a sale to the CTO of a company can mean making Oracle the standard database product for the entire company. Contrast this with the grassroots sales approach, where a sales team has to figure out the whole organization and has to make an individual sale to each particular division. Each one of those sales can take significantly longer than a single sale to a CTO. Further, any divisional purchase can be thrown out by a purchase that is

made higher up in the organization. Winning over an organization is easiest, and your product is most secure, with a
top-down selling process. A salesperson from Ingres told
me that several times she had sold an Ingres database (a
competitive product to Oracle) into a division of a large
company and was beginning to work her way into other
divisions of the same company when the word came down
that management had made a strategic commitment to
Oracle and that all Ingres projects would be cancelled.

Switching cost

A great long-term benefit of completing a corporate
standardization sale is the huge cost of switching away from
technology that is already in use. Once all of a company's
information is managed by Oracle software, the expense
and effort associated with moving to a competitor's product
is very high. On the implementation side, there is the cost
of learning a new product, developing new applications, and
then somehow converting all of the information from a
system that the company relies on every day. These expenses
can far outweigh the entire purchase cost of the Oracle
system or any system that would try to replace an Oracle
system. On the emotional level, a lot of employee time and
effort goes into making applications based on Oracle function successfully, and walking away from them is difficult.

Avoid ugly details

Because Oracle sales executives call into an organization
at "the 50,000 foot level," they also talk to corporate executives at "the 50,000 foot level." That means that they do not
have to get caught up in the technical details of the database
and the competition; rather, they have to understand and

discuss how Oracle software will have a positive impact on the customer's business. A detailed technical evaluation of the product can often lead to a time-consuming competitive situation that a salesperson wants to avoid. By calling on the highest levels in the customer organization, an Oracle salesperson can promote the explicit business benefits of an Oracle database. Taking the high road, they can often deliver a faster sale by selling strategy.

Demo

Another critical ingredient required to sell at the very highest levels of an organization is an attractive product demonstration. Senior executives are not dumb, they are just short on time. Oracle does an excellent job of setting up Oracle presales engineers with compelling demonstrations of different applications of Oracle technology. This allows an Oracle sales executive to crystallize the business benefit and power of an Oracle product into a short and visually appealing demonstration.

Internal support for the Oracle purchase

One of the most powerful elements of selling high is the ongoing support that Oracle can count on from the executive who made the purchase. That person made a significant financial and personal commitment to Oracle technology and strategy, therefore, that person has a strong interest in seeing Oracle deployed in a positive way. Needless to say, there are certainly going to be implementation problems in a database that includes an entire company's information, yet many of Oracle's competitors whose database was bought by a division head have been thrown out of accounts when these shortcomings were exposed to upper management. In contrast, an Oracle database is typically purchased by upper management, so upper management is more sympathetic to problems that arise from a project that includes its technology.

Executives sell to executives

Oracle's goal is to sell high in an organization, and every one of Oracle management team is prepared to support the effort. Oracle's CFO spends several weeks a quarter out in the field selling Oracle financial applications. He makes himself available to Oracle sales representatives who can set meetings up for him with CFOs of Fortune 500 companies. In those meetings, he is a very effective and credible Oracle representative because, to the customer, he is a peer. He uses Oracle products. But he is also a good salesperson, asking questions such as: "I can close my books in three days at the end of the year—can you do that?" and "I run my business on Oracle, why don't you?"

The only negative associated with the selling high strategy is that it requires salespeople who are often expensive to hire. However, organizations with a high-end product can derive these and many more benefits from making an investment in their own sales force so that they have the tools, the story, and the support necessary to sell to an executive.

Marketing to Enterprise Customers—Seminar Power!

Oracle sells database software to large corporate customers. These organizations are corporate America's elite and they are used to being treated that way. They expect to have the sales process catered to them.

Oracle didn't invent the seminar, but the company did elevate it to something of an art form. Today, companies like Microsoft are copying Oracle's strategy. For years, if you were a Fortune 500 executive, there was always a seminar coming to a stylish venue near you. A number of elements to Oracle's seminar program made it unique and extremely successful:

- Oracle's seminars were not presented as sales pitches, but rather as an opportunity to learn about relational database technology and the industry as a whole. Oracle positioned its talk as the kind of educational opportunity that a prospect might have to pay for if Oracle were not so benevolent.
- Oracle's events were always held in the niccst hotel in the area, which was both consistent with Oracle's image and helped to attract senior people to attend the event.
- Oracle always served food at the event. At morning seminars executives were treated to croissant, Danish, and coffee, while and at afternoon events they enjoyed fresh cookies and soda.
- Oracle always promised a live product demonstration.

Sales prospects were recruited to attend seminars mostly by direct mail. Oracle would target regional audiences approximately three months before a seminar was due to come to town, and the telemarketing group would call prospects to get as many as possible from the mailing list to attend.

At the seminar, executives were escorted into a main ballroom where there was one large screen and rows of tables and chairs set up. In the back, Oracle sometimes had tables with third-party partners demonstrating their solutions. After a brief introduction of the local sales team, an Oracle executive presented an overview of relational database technology and the industry as a whole. The presenter then took questions before an Oracle sales engineering consultant moved into a compelling demonstration of Oracle products. A second question and answer period followed. Before and after each of the presentations, attendees were free to enjoy refreshments and mingle with Oracle employees.

Oracle's seminars were a fantastic lever to many of the points in the sales process. It gave local salespeople something of a fallback position for a customer that they couldn't sell right away but whom they wanted to keep on the hook. It gave Oracle telesales staff a reason to call a new prospect without trying to sell them something right away. It provided a fantastic way to qualify a prospect because anyone willing to sit through a three-hour presentation of Oracle technology must be somewhat interested. And it set up a temporary local demonstration center for prospects in areas where there was no local Oracle office. All in all, the seminar program was a critical part of Oracle's early sales success where there was as much evangelizing as selling happening.

Any organization that sells to corporate America can take advantage of the seminar program model. If the cost and effort to put one on is daunting, seminars shared with partners may be a little bit more difficult to organize but can be less expensive. Either way, a company can get the same benefits that Oracle did: having a non-sales reason to call a customer and a limited-time opportunity for a customer to come and see a new product.

Sell Into Vertical Industries

In the early 1990s, Oracle stepped back and took a look at profiles of the types of customers buying Oracle software. As a result of this exercise, the company realized that the bulk of its customers fell into one of eight industry categories, known in the high-tech industry as "vertical markets" because they are in industries other than technology. These vertical markets included manufacturing, health care, telecommunications, and others.

Wanting both to grow into new markets and to dominate markets it was already in, Oracle decided to add a sales team devoted to vertical markets to its existing regional sales force. The theory was simple: If Oracle could devote staff to developing a deep understanding of what customers at, for example, major airlines needed from Oracle, the company could target product, marketing, and salespeople specifically at the airline industry and win the entire vertical area. And Oracle could build marketing that directly addressed the needs of airline customers and technology that was truly focused on a customer need.

Oracle's implementation of the vertical sales force concept included specialists in each of the following vertical market industries including:

- Travel and Transportation (TNT)
- Manufacturing
- Aerospace
- Health Care
- Mining and Exploration

In many ways, creating a vertical sales force was a natural extension of the origin of selling at Oracle, which was highly customer focused. In each industry, Oracle attended trade shows and created customer success stories detailing how leaders of each industry used Oracle to improve their business.

Oracle's first attempt to create vertical sales teams, however, was far from perfect because when the teams were rolled out, the regional sales representatives were still responsible for their geographic territories except for companies that fell into one of the targeted vertical categories. Those companies were now served by the vertical sales-people who were based at Oracle's headquarters in California. The following negative results ensued:

Regional sales stopped chasing accounts

In some areas, the regional salespeople adopted the new organization quite literally. The regional representatives immediately ignored accounts they had been working for years, knowing that they would not get paid for any software sold into that account. The vertical sales force, back at headquarters, was slow to take control of all of the vertical accounts, thus many prospects with ready needs to buy Oracle software were dropped.

Several people calling on the same account

In other areas, the regional representatives did not embrace the new organization at all. They continued to call on customers in vertical accounts even after the vertical sales force had also contacted the account. It was unclear from the customer's perspective how to buy Oracle software, and a lot of effort was wasted internally at Oracle arguing over who was responsible for an account.

Creation of a huge expense item

Oracle created new positions with vertical sales, and those who filled them were redundant to the existing sales force. The added expense was great and immediate and would not be offset until some later time when the new staff could sustain itself with the incremental revenue that it booked.

Vertical accounts managed from the West Coast

One of the tremendous advantages that Oracle had always had in selling against the competition was that Oracle invested early in a large number of regional offices. This gave Oracle representatives the ability to have frequent meetings in an effort to build strong relationships with prospective and existing clients. Having most of the vertical sales force located in California was bad for account presence, particularly when an account had become accustomed to a very high level of personal service.

Sales subject to industry trends

Unlike regional salespeople who found opportunities in all industry areas, the vertical sales force suffered from problems that were specific to their vertical areas. For example, in the early 1990s the airline industry was going through a viciously competitive time where all of the airlines spent their time and money fighting each other, not investing in infrastructure. The Travel and Transport vertical sales group, focused on the airlines, quickly found that it had nothing to sell because the airlines simply were too distracted at the time.

After two years of competition, Oracle realized it needed a better solution, a model that would reconcile the vertical sales force with the rest of field sales. The company also realized at that time that it had a second sales issue to resolve. How was Oracle going to sell its application products, which had finally been completed after years in development? The solution was obvious.

In general terms, Oracle converted the vertical sales team into a sales force for Oracle's database application software products. The Oracle applications were inherently vertically targeted, so selling them was similar to selling the database into specific vertical accounts. But instead of being competitive with the traditional Oracle sales force, the applications salespeople were complementary. For example, after an Oracle sales representative sold an Oracle database to a major manufacturer, an Oracle applications sales representative could go back to the same customer with an application for manufacturing inventory management that worked with the Oracle database. Just as the software added functionality to an Oracle database and as such enjoyed a cooperative relationship, so now did applications salespersons with the rest of Oracle sales.

The lesson from Oracle's experience is that there is a tremendous amount of leverage to be gained by developing overwhelming selling power and targeting a particular vertical industry. More important, however, an organization must coordinate its sales approach to those industries so that it is complementary with other sales activities going on concurrently. This can harness your selling power.

Sales Today Make Markets Tomorrow

There are many factors that play into how aggressive a company chooses to be in its selling practices. Product cycles, market size, market growth, and competition all play into that decision. In the mid- to late 1980s, Oracle looked at the huge and largely untouched database market, at several competitors who were roughly the size of Oracle, and at the immaturity of all of the products that were available, and decided that Oracle's goal would be to gain market share at all costs.

The head of sales at the time was focused on winning customers at all of the Fortune 100 companies. His assumption was that if Oracle could satisfy all of these large, demanding, high-profile organizations, he would be able to move down to smaller companies and win easily based on his success with the Fortune 100. There were posters all over the Oracle sales offices listing the target companies. The ones that Oracle had won were tagged. Those that Oracle wanted to win were highlighted.

In addition to focusing on the target market, he introduced a new sales tactic to drive Oracle's pursuit of market share. The concept was called "The CAP." A former sales representative who worked during this time simplified the concept by telling me what the customer heard: "If you buy databases for ten computers this year, and promise to buy databases for fifty computers over the next five years, we'll give them all to you at the special rate that we have now. Prices are going up; it's the fourth quarter and we are ready to deal."

These were very compelling deals to customers because if they made a commitment to buy Oracle this year, they had set a company direction that included Oracle technology and would likely have to buy more databases in the upcoming years. For customers, locking Oracle into a low price now was very appealing, and some of the deals were delivering fantastically low prices. While 50 percent off Oracle's list price was pretty standard, discounts now approached 80 percent based on the stature of a particular customer and the volume they were willing to buy.

In terms of building market share for Oracle, this tactic was brilliant for three reasons:

1. Standardization. It gave a customer a compelling cost reason to make a standardization decision on Oracle.
2. Large deals. It gave the Oracle sales force a powerful tool for elevating the sales discussion because it involved a long-term corporate choice and for closing a bigger deal than they might have first found at a customer site.
3. Revenue reporting flexibility. It gave Oracle's accounting team a powerful lever to boost the revenue numbers that it reported.

The third reason, although subtle, is the most important advantage of the CAP. In the simple example described above, Oracle booked the revenue for the ten databases that it delivered in the first year. The important thing was that Oracle also had the option to book the fifty "future" deliveries at the same time it booked the ten current deliveries. This enabled Oracle to choose what kind of revenue number and what kind of growth it wanted to show to the marketplace. Of course, Oracle chose to show huge growth, which was critical to creating the perception with both customers and competitors that Oracle owned the database market.

While I am not suggesting that any company knowingly overstate revenues, I want to highlight that Oracle did everything that it could to create the perception of owning its market. As was proven out, the CAP did later cause problems for Oracle both in terms of a business and a perception problem.

Oracle spent years working off the CAPs

Many of the customers who wisely took advantage of the steep price cuts offered in the CAPs had no need to sign license agreements for any more software from Oracle for the duration of that CAP—up to five years. During that time, that customer's sales representative had to go find other opportunities to sell Oracle, while still making sure that the customers who had paid for CAPs were satisfied.

The DSO (Days Sales Outstanding) was huge

Even though Oracle had booked the revenue from a CAP, it was months or years until Oracle would actually be able to receive the money. Analysts on Wall Street look at a variety of numbers when they evaluate a company's business. When they saw Oracle's Days Sales Outstanding (DSO) number, they knew the company had been aggressive about how it had chosen to recognize its deals. The analysts knew that if Oracle growth slowed at all, the DSO would catch up with the company because Oracle would not have cash access to all of the revenue that it claimed. Further, the large DSO number meant that the likelihood of customers defaulting on their commitments to Oracle was high, and when that happened Oracle would have to write off as bad debt some of the revenue it had previously claimed. This was one of the big factors that caused the Oracle stock sell off in 1990 when the company had its only losing quarter to date—an event that I later refer to as "The Crash."

Bad accounting

It became obvious to the accountants that Oracle was living on borrowed time, and twice in the early 1990s Oracle had to make some significant earnings restatement announcements.

People who talk about the CAP issue today are still polarized on it. Some say that the CAP was one of the factors that caused Oracle to crash in 1990. Others say that the CAP is one of the weapons that won Oracle ownership of the database market. Either way, it is a tactic that is unique to Oracle and certainly had a big impact on the company. Companies today have much less flexibility with respect to revenue reporting because of the creative accounting that went on at Oracle and other high-technology companies in the 1980s.

Promote Your Vision

In 1989, Oracle sold something brilliant. It wasn't a revolutionary new technology or a new channel—it was much simpler. Oracle focused its incredible selling power on a vision!

An employee in Oracle's core technology group authored a white paper on an architecture called SQL* (pronounced sequel star). All of Oracle's products were based on the SQL database language and all the products had names like SQL*Report (a report generating product) and SQL*Forms (a database interface product), but this white paper didn't describe any real products that customers could buy. Instead, it described an architecture.

The SQL* architecture described a vision of how an Oracle database could be spread across countless different computers, connected by different networks and accessed by a huge range of different kinds of workstations. The paper explained the architecture in more detail than just a glossy brochure, discussing how all of the different databases would communicate to make sure that all the information could be accessible by anyone in the organization, that access would be secure and that the data would be safe from any glitches in any of the computers or in the network.

At the time, the paper had only little relevance to Oracle's actual product offering. As a result, the whole concept of writing a white paper for something that Oracle did not have seemed ridiculous to me. Customers would call wanting to buy SQL*. What would I tell them? "Send me a check and I'll send you another copy of that paper." It seemed preposterous that Oracle would waste its time promoting something that it could not sell.

I could not have been more wrong. In fact, the company could sell SQL*. Or more specifically, the salespeople could use the vision of SQL* to open a conversation with a potential customer about the possibilities for the future of information management. Based on that conversation, a salesperson could sell the existing Oracle products with the promise that Oracle would be working to extend the product line to deliver on all of the functionality and benefits of SQL* and, consequently, deliver a fantastic solution to the customer. The salesperson made the initial database sale with the then current version and had an excuse to come back and sell more product later. The competition paled by comparison, appearing to be short on vision and direction.

Oracle was not the only organization to define and sell an architecture. IBM also released its description of SNA (Systems Network Architecture), which outlined a framework for how all IBM machines could interact and communicate. The result was equally as powerful. The market as a whole believed that IBM had a vision for how to make its diverse product line exchange information, even when IBM did not have the products to support it.

In an industry like technology where customers' expectations are set for constant change, it's now imperative to sell a future while still delivering current products. But I believe that this is an effective strategy for any product development company because publishing a vision can be as positive internally as externally. Not only does it share with the rest of the company the vision for future products, it lets employees know that they are part of something big, something with a future. And at the very heart, it can force a management team to come to agreement on what direction they will take the company in the coming years.

CHAPTER SIX

Customer Relationships

A FEW YEARS AGO, UNITED AIRLINES RAN AN ADVERTISING CAMPAIGN THAT EVERYONE IN BUSINESS COULD APPRECIATE. It featured a sales team sitting around a conference room table with the president of the company addressing them. The president talked about how well the sales team was communicating with customers using the phone, fax, and e-mail, but the company was still losing business. The president then reached into his pocket and handed out airline tickets to each sales representative. The message was clear: Visit your customers!

Visit Your Customers

Over the years, Oracle learned how to make large corporate customers successful with leading-edge, sophisticated technology. It began with the inclusion of customers in the product development process. Yet Oracle would not have been successful had it let the customer relationship stop there. Today, Oracle still uses a number of tactics to stay close to its customers once they have purchased an Oracle product.

Establish local offices

Oracle invested early in U.S. and international offices in order to stay close to its customers. When customers needed something, they didn't have to worry about dialing long distance or calculating time zone differences in order to reach an Oracle sales representative. In turn, a sales representative could set up more casual meetings, say over breakfast or lunch, to catch up with customers and hear their feedback about Oracle products.

Set up executive briefing centers

Oracle also has a formal executive briefing center for customers and prospects visiting the company's headquarters in Redwood Shores, California. The briefing center, primarily used for day-long meetings, features the latest in audio-visual technology and serves as a showcase of Oracle technology. Customers who visit the briefing center are treated to first-class accommodations, complete with catered food from one of Oracle's chefs, as they listen to the Oracle pitch and meet Oracle's executive team.

Host local seminars and developer conferences

As discussed in the previous chapter, Oracle also maintains contact with customers through its regular, multi-city seminar program. Additionally, the company hosts an annual user/developer conference, now called "Oracle Open World," to attract customers and prospects. Always held in a desirable destination at a nice hotel and featuring good food and entertainment, the three-day event includes sessions hosted by Oracle developers, customers, and product marketing managers. The conference not only provides education, but it is an opportunity for additional Oracle employees to meet Oracle customers face-to-face.

Talk with Your Customers

After I completed Oracle Boot Camp, a week-long indoctrination into Oracle culture and technology that I will discuss in a subsequent chapter, I started as a product manager in Oracle's Desktop division. I was responsible for the desktop network products: the software that lets a personal computer get database information from a big mainframe server. On my first day, I was presented with my first assignment: to talk with a customer who was using my product. The customer was American Express.

Dutifully, I called and explained my product responsibilities. Boy, did I get an earful! The contact told me that his salesperson had promised a piece of software to him months ago and it was a critical piece of the implementation he was doing for a department in American Express. He hadn't been able to get any good answers from Oracle and when the hell would I get him what he needed?! Clearly, the project was on the line and so was his job.

From this conversation on my very first day at work, I had been exposed to four important things:

- A specific project that included my software
- A particular customer environment (computers, network, and software) that included my software
- The understanding that Oracle products were being used for mission-critical applications
- The significance that Oracle products had in people's lives

While my first customer interaction was difficult, the experience was invaluable. Not only did I appreciate the importance of the products that we were working on, I also immediately understood how they would be used in the real world.

Watch Your Customers Use Your Product

Oracle promotes a high degree of customer interaction. When I was responsible for a development group, I made everyone in the group spend a week answering calls on the customer support lines. While it was difficult to drag people away from their desks, the experience they got from working in support was valuable. They were exposed to the same types of issues that I was on my first day and many more. Not only did they experience the technical issues that people were facing with our products, they also understood a customer's frustration with a difficult installation procedure or misleading documentation. And perhaps most importantly, they could share in a customer's exhilaration when a problem was solved and the product worked correctly.

Understanding how customers use a product is important to Oracle because it impacts every aspect of the development process, including:

- Deciding whether to develop a product or not in the first place
- What it will look like
- What it will do
- How the installation will work
- What platforms it will run on

- How it will be documented
- How easy it will be to support
- What applications it will be used to support

A development head in another group told me, "I would go and visit customers and sometimes it amazed me what people were doing with our product. I would be surprised at the size of a deployment or the amount of effort that people were putting into the infrastructure around an Oracle deployment. When I went back to work on the product, I knew that I was not just building a toy."

In addition to product marketing, Oracle's kernel group also has a clear and specific mission with respect to customers. Its mission, described to me by a senior architect, is "to retrieve the customer's data and never to have a down database. It is that simple." He continued, "Having a mission statement that simple gives everyone clarity of vision. If there is a down database, we stop everything. That allows everyone to make the right decision without having to consult their manager."

The benefits that Oracle employees reap from staying close to their customers are not specific to the technology world. An organization that exposes all of its members to customers using its products will see how each employee, based on his or her own responsibility, takes customer experiences and interactions and comes back to the office with new insights and ideas.

Help Customers Use Your Product

The first release of Oracle was Version 2. It was early technology, delivered only to a small number of customers. It was not just a new product; it was a whole new approach to managing information. And it required a great deal of training to teach system administrators and programmers how to use it, as well as frequent support interaction when something broke or didn't work as expected.

Although Oracle understood that the advancement of both market understanding and its product maturing would happen slowly, the company was determined to make sure that customers understood the product, used the product, and were successful with the product.

To that end, Oracle placed technical support engineers in field sales offices where they could be closer to customers. This early decentralized support model gave the salespeople control over what level of support a particular customer received. The salespeople were also able to insure that customers with compelling applications or high-profile customers who were desirable reference accounts would use their Oracle software and be happy with it.

The "field" support engineers spent a great deal of time at customer sites, teaching users and programmers how to take advantage of an Oracle database, evangelizing the benefits of the SQL language and the benefits of the relational model. Equally as important, the support engineers received valuable information directly from customers about problems encountered, as well as examples of applications using the technology, which the support engineers brought back to Oracle. Using this information, designers at headquarters could plan the next product with features that would better serve these applications. As a result, support engineers in the field served as designers' eyes and ears into a variety of customers.

It is important to note here that these field support engineers were people who wore many hats. In hiring them, Oracle had to find team players that could handle the wide range of tasks that would be expected of them. In the course of any given week, a support engineer could expect to do any or all of the following:

Technical training

An Oracle field engineer had to be able to explain how to use an Oracle database to every person within a customer organization who would have to interact with it. This included the detailed system programming expertise that was required to build an application to access an Oracle database, as well as the higher level explanation of how an end user enters information into an Oracle database or runs a report to get information from the database.

Fixing a bug

Early versions of Oracle were optimized for immediate release to the customer, not necessarily for exhaustive quality assurance. The chance that a customer would find a bug, or system difficulty, in an Oracle product was reasonably high by today's standards. As a result, field support engineers had to understand the architecture and implementation of Oracle well enough to walk into a customer site and be able to fix a problem that had been identified.

Performing a benchmark

Database performance is critical to any application. Many implementations of Oracle are in areas of "real-time" access such as the use of an automated teller machine. After you make a request to withdraw $20, you must wait while a database, such as Oracle's, processes the transaction. There is a great deal of time and effort devoted to measuring database response time and optimizing it, and this process is called benchmarking. Benchmarks are often performed against a competitive product when a customer is evaluating purchasing options, or they can be done to optimize Oracle operation for a particular customer application. Field support engineers are expected to handle both.

Writing an application

Early on, the Oracle database had no graphical or end user interface. It was simply an engine for managing data, and it was left to customers to write the user interface themselves. That is, unless they paid Oracle for a field support engineer to help them create the application. This function has since become the Oracle Consulting Group's responsibility, but in the beginning it was handled by Oracle field support engineers.

Explaining Oracle technology to a prospective customer

Selling Oracle has always involved some discussion of the technology. The field salespeople that Oracle hired from the beginning were specialists in calling on senior levels in the organization, establishing a broad base of contacts and putting together big deals. They did not have—nor were they expected to have—expertise in the technical implementation of Oracle products. Sales representatives relied on their field support engineer to back them up when they got into a technical discussion with a prospective customer.

Laying out the database

Before the relational model and SQL, every database stored information in a huge grid, similar to a spreadsheet. One of the reasons that the relational model and SQL was so successful was that, unlike the old model, it was flexible in how it handled information, was efficient in storage space, and was easier to manage. Using the relational model, users had more control over how their data was stored and how to organize it, but the new approach required some understanding in order to reap the benefits. A well-structured relational database could easily outshine a traditional database, while a poorly designed relational database would likely never do what a customer wanted. The field support engineers spent time with customers explaining relational design and stepping them through the layout of their data in the database.

Migrating data

Oracle knew that once it had a company's critical information stored in an Oracle database it would have a much better chance at retaining a customer. The hard part was getting that information into Oracle's software in the first place. For companies that started fresh with Oracle, it was easier. They just had to enter the data into the database by hand as it came in. The majority of companies, however, had information already stored on another platform, perhaps in an IBM mainframe database. It was the responsibility of Oracle field support engineers to figure out how to move that information from the IBM mainframe into the Oracle database, making sure that none of it got lost or corrupted along the way.

A comprehensive list of tasks performed by Oracle's field support engineers could take up the rest of this book, but quantity is not the point of this discussion. The point is that providing local support in the field can be a great tactic for growing a business early on. It is certainly one that Oracle used in a proactive manner.

Oracle's field support engineers also each had a list of the customers for whom they were responsible. The rule was if the field support engineers' phones weren't ringing, they were supposed to call the customers on their list just to check in and make sure that all was well. In some cases, the call was very brief. In other cases, the support engineer was able to avert a problem before it even became problem. And sometimes the field support engineer was even able to sell the customer more products or services based on where the customer was in the process.

Having field support engineers was more costly than setting up a centralized support organization and the number of employees had to grow as the business grew, yet the benefit to Oracle early on was great. One of the original support engineers told me, "The system worked up to when Oracle had about 1,000 customers per office. I was able to take care of 250 customers myself and there were three other field support people in my office who also did the same thing."

However, faced with a rapidly growing customer base and a very high cost of support, as well as other structural issues in the field sales force, Oracle realized that it had accomplished what it needed to with the field support engineers. In 1986, the company centralized its support organization into the headquarters location.

Looking back, had Oracle not placed support engineers in the field early on, the entire company could easily have failed. Certainly, some customers would have purchased the product, but due to its complex nature, they would likely have been unsatisfied or unsuccessful with it absent the local field support. Customers would have gotten frustrated and they would have moved on to other technology. Having support in the field was Oracle's way of insuring the initial sale took hold at a customer site.

Now that Oracle's products are more mature and have been implemented at thousands of sites throughout the world, the centralized model of support suits the company and its customers well. In many areas, there are now third-party organizations that provide Oracle support on an ongoing basis. And while Oracle is still attentive to its customers' needs and the company still sends support engineers to visit customer sites, longer-term, more specialized, customer engagements are now handled by the Oracle Consulting Group on a contract basis.

It is up an individual company, and perhaps more importantly, the stage that company is at (early or more mature) to determine whether a decentralized or centralized method of support is more beneficial.

Regardless of the choice, any business can apply the same strategy that Oracle used to rollout its products by keeping in mind that the more complex the product, the more early adopters need local and immediate attention to be successful. Once customers are successful, they will provide a fantastic base of references, feedback on the product, and application stories that can help win over countless more customers.

Set Realistic Expectations

An Oracle developer who had a lot of customer contact remembers, "The only difference between a happy customer and an irate one is how their expectations were set in the beginning."

In the early days, Oracle only did a good job of setting customer expectations some of the time. Today, it is much better—but the company learned its lesson the hard way.

The first versions of the Oracle database were revolutionary new technology, but they certainly were not ready to be the basis on which a company's business was run. Oracle's first CFO told me, "The people who did well with the Oracle technology early on were the people who bought it and put it in the back room. They knew that relational technology was coming and they wanted to be ready for it. They wanted to check it out. GM and Bell both had research labs where early versions of Oracle were installed and both benefited tremendously from it." However, other initial customers who had different expectations for the product, ended up disappointed.

Based on criticism from early customers, Oracle was forced to create an Oracle User Group and hold annual User Group meetings. The first User Group, which met in 1986, merely provided unhappy customers a forum to vent their frustrations and demands. As Oracle User Groups began to spring up around the country, Oracle developers and marketing people put more effort into listening to the issues that came up at the meetings, which translated directly into fixing problems in the company's products and processes. In part as a result of its User Groups, today Oracle makes it a point to align promises with deliveries.

Once Oracle heard customers' feedback, set expectations, and fixed many of the problems, the User Groups became some of Oracle's best references. As an Oracle person who attended several Oracle User Group meetings told me, "I swear this happened three times: a new user would come in with a complaint about a product and the other users would shut them down by saying, 'No. You're not using it right! You don't know what you are talking about!'."

It is always good policy to deal with customers in a proactive manner, especially in an industry like technology where products are shipped early and often. By setting expectations correctly in the beginning, you can avoid having to patch up problems later on.

CHAPTER SEVEN

Crush Your Competition

IN THE LATE 1970s, ORACLE WAS NOT THE ONLY COMPANY TO RECOGNIZE THE MARKET NEED FOR DATABASE SOFTWARE. At about the same time Oracle started, two other companies were created with the same mission. Other, more established, technology vendors joined the market soon after. What made Oracle stand out, however, was its strategy of attacking and, subsequently, crushing the competition.

Five Steps to Attacking Your Competition

Oracle's stance toward any competitor was clear and direct: "Annihilate them." Many times Larry Ellison used the old Genghis Khan adage, "It is not enough that I succeed; all others must fail."

To achieve Larry's goal, Oracle developed five steps to attacking any competitor the company might encounter. These tactics, still employed by Oracle today, include:

1. Inventing a simple characterization of a competitive company
2. Making sure the characterization is credible

3. Turning a competitor's own positioning against them, if possible
4. Communicating the characterization to everyone in your organization
5. Making sure that a customer never buys from a vendor branded with your characterization.

Using these tactics, Oracle aggressively attacked Ingres (originally Relational Technologies, Inc.) and Informix Software, both of whom built products that competed head-on with Oracle. Once the market was more established, Oracle focused its attention on newcomer, Sybase, which was also formed to offer database products and services. Further, Oracle took on several of the major hardware companies including IBM and Digital Equipment Corporation (DEC) that had undertaken projects to build their own database software for their own particular platforms.

Cut Off the Oxygen

In the mid-1980s, Informix was larger than Oracle in sales. Oracle launched a two-year "Cut Off The Oxygen" to Informix campaign. The campaign included a detailed competitive understanding of Informix's products and specific initiatives to combat them, such as:

- Purchasing, installing, and conducting a detailed evaluation of every commercially available Informix product
- Writing and distributing internal competitive bulletins

- Aggressively advertising comparative product features, performance, and benefits
- Providing additive incentive bonuses to salespeople who beat Informix
- Creating "Cut Off the Oxygen" T-shirts that carried a graphic of an old-style diver on the bottom of the ocean with "Informix" written on his chest. His air line was about to be chomped, just above his head, by a large shark that had "Oracle" written on it.
- Recruiting people from Informix, increasing Oracle's personnel numbers and knowledge of the competition, while simultaneously decreasing Informix's numbers and the morale of those who remained at the competitor
- Involving executive management in Informix competitive situations
- Recruiting third parties working with Informix or distributing their products
- Supplying press with competitive product comparisons
- Launching the "Where is Phil White (Informix president) Campaign?" which tracked Phil's travel schedule and sent an Oracle sales team every place Phil went.

Today Informix is less than one tenth the size of Oracle, its stock price is low, and the company's recently purchased Illustra product has not been well received by the market. The Oracle offensive has taken its toll.

In the case of Informix and every other competitive vendor, Oracle battled relentlessly, not just for its own piece, but for the entire database market.

Pigeonholing Individual Competitors

Oracle's strategy was to look at each competitor individually and figure out the one reason that vendor could be made to look unacceptable to a potential buyer. Then Oracle propagated that message throughout the sales and marketing organizations, so that whenever anyone from Oracle was asked about a particular competitor, the answer was the same. People outside of the company who heard it enough began to believe it, and a legacy was born that a competitor would have to respond to in a hurry. Here are a few of the competitors that Oracle has overcome and the corresponding pigeonhole Oracle stuck them in:

Ingres

This database company was started by a team of professors at the University of California, Berkeley. They hired a large number of Berkeley computer science graduates and even located the company close to campus so that it could continue to benefit from the talent at the university. Early on, it was widely recognized that Ingres had better technology than Oracle, but Oracle labeled the product a "Research Project," knowing that no serious information technology manager could afford to bet his or her business on a college research project.

When Ingres finally closed its doors in 1994, Oracle recruiters were outside with stacks of employment applications and long lists of available positions at Oracle.

Sybase

In 1987, when Sybase was just starting up, people at Oracle showed up at headquarters wearing buttons that read simply "Sybase: Crib Death."

Almost by its own doing, Sybase was tagged "The erector set company." The solution that Sybase offered a customer was always cobbled together using Sybase's database product combined with partner tools and applications. Oracle sales representatives would ask a prospective customer who was considering Sybase "Who are you going to call when you have a problem?" and claimed that making all of the pieces fit together would take lots of programming time. It made Sybase look like a real technician's database. For a while, Sybase encouraged the categorization, wanting to prove that its technology was serious, but later tried to change the image. It could be said that Sybase's (failed) acquisition of Gain and its (expensive) acquisition of Powersoft both represented efforts to change the perception that its solution was incomplete.

The most recent entrant into the database market, Sybase was also the last to find itself in the Oracle cross hairs. Sybase won some high-visibility deals from Oracle during its early days, but after ten years of competing with Oracle, Sybase began hemorrhaging people and customers and has fallen behind on product releases.

Informix

Although Informix has had many good years of sales and still enjoys a very good relationship with its resellers, Oracle always niched Informix as being second best, referring to the company as "Always a bridesmaid but never a bride." This moniker stuck because Informix was never as aggressive as Oracle in making its database run on a wide range of platforms or at getting huge performance out of its database. This tactic was very successful when Oracle sales representatives called on Fortune 500 customers, who were always sure to buy the premium product in every area.

In addition to posting product release schedules in the hallways, Oracle posted blow-ups of Oracle advertisements that ran in trade publications. These ads were always combative in nature, often including bar chart comparisons of Oracle performance versus the competition. It was a constant reminder to employees that it is a battle, and Oracle has high expectations of success.

Ashton-Tate/dBase

When Oracle decided to adapt its database to run on the PC platform, Ashton-Tate's dBase was the popular incumbent offering. Unfortunately for Ashton-Tate, dBase did not run anywhere other than the PC platform. The underlying computer running dBase, the PC, could not support any large number of users, and although dBase was very easy to use and well built for the PC, Oracle pigeonholed the offering as "a toy"—not industrial strength enough for any serious application and, as such, unsuitable for a business.

Oracle persecuted any company even thinking about the database area. The company's advertisements in 1988 showed an F-16 jet with an Oracle logo shooting down a triplane with a dBase logo. The text at the top of the ad read, "Oracle: The last RDBMS (Relational Database Management System)."

Cullinet

Cullinet had been around for much longer than Oracle, and while the company had a great deal of the maturity that Oracle needed, the aggressive Oracle sales representatives characterized Cullinet as being an "old company with old technology." This pitch was well received within the

Fortune 500, who considered themselves to be leaders and innovators.

IBM, HP, DEC

Any hardware company who wrote its own database software for its computer platform was blatantly exposed to Oracle. Oracle had bet its business on making its software portable and, therefore, making the computer that ran it a simple commodity. IBM, HP, DEC, and others had created fine database software products for their own computers, but when the Oracle sales representative came in and asked a prospective customer, "What if next year a different manufacturer comes out with a much faster/cheaper computer and you want to start buying those? You'll be stuck unless you buy Oracle, which runs on them all!" It was a compelling question and response, made so because each year a different manufacturer did have a faster/cheaper computer and many of the Fortune 500 companies began to purchase machines from a number of different manufacturers. All of the computer vendors were characterized by Oracle as being proprietary by their very nature.

After many years of losing market share to Oracle on its own computers, in 1991 DEC offered its product, named RDB, free to any of its customers. Oracle caught wind of this offer before it was made public and countered with an advertisement that said, "Even if RDB was Free, You Couldn't Afford It." After Oracle had shown DEC that it could sell Oracle software to DEC's customers while DEC was offering RDB for free, DEC sold its database software staff to Oracle.

Pinpointing the enemy and treating competition like warfare earned Larry Ellison a caricature of Genghis Khan in an article in *Upside* magazine. It also earned him complete dominance of the information management category.

Companies that want to own a market can learn from Oracle's example. Actively seek out the competitive targets that your business wants to overpower and attack them every way possible. Oracle paid salespeople double commission for any sale they won where they replaced Ingres, Informix, or Sybase with Oracle. And Larry's animosity toward these companies was constant, obvious, and public. When targeting the competition, remember the Oracle mantra: "It is not enough that we succeed, all others must fail."

Document Victories

The enemy is the competition, and Oracle goes to great lengths to focus the company on the enemy. In the late 1980s, as part of the campaign to "Cut Off the Oxygen" to Informix, Oracle offered T-shirts to anyone who played a part in beating Informix in a sales situation. Some people considered the shirts, featuring a shark, to be excessively violent, until they got one themselves. Aside from being true "spoils of war," the T-shirts prompted a great deal of information exchange. It was almost expected that other employees would ask the wearer of such a shirt how he or she was able to overcome Informix. Soon, details of the battle ensued and "war stories" about late nights and cans of Coke consumed during database tuning in a competitive benchmark situation were common.

As a result of these kinds of encounters, Oracle "competitive bulletins" were born. Competitive bulletins were at least six pages of tables comparing feature versus feature with anecdotal text describing competitive situations where Oracle employees had encountered a particular competitor. The bulletins were developed by Oracle marketing, but they also included specific technical information about how Oracle performed against competitive products in a controlled benchmark situation.

While I was at Oracle, my manager actually developed a formula for assembling a huge amount of information about a competitor and publishing it, so that every salesperson was armed with company and product information on each competitor. He explained his secret as follows: "You write the complete competitive bulletin—how we win, how we lose—and then you do the following: You rip off the last pages, the 'How We Get Beaten by the Competition' section and hand it to engineering. That's the beginning of the specification for the next revision of the product. Then you hand the rest of the competitive bulletin with all the comparisons to the sales guys and you write 'Company Confidential' all over it, just to make sure the sales guys will hand them out to customers."

The result was fantastic. Marketing received e-mail notes from all over the company about experiences that other people had with competitive products. Marketing collected those and released additional competitive bulletins. Today, there is a whole team at Oracle devoted to just that function.

In most companies, collecting competitive information begins as an ad hoc process. Employees share information found on Web sites, learned in customer meetings, or at trade shows. However, adding structure to the process in the form of regular bulletins or e-mails can be invaluable for winning deals over the competition. Companies that are serious about taking on the competition head-to-head generally find it worthwhile to invest in an employee or group of employees to conduct competitive research or they task individual product managers in marketing to distribute information. Either way, arming your employees with information about the competition does help win deals.

Fight Opponents on Your Terms

Customers evaluate products on a number of criteria. When you buy a car, for example, you don't just look at the cost, you consider its color, engine size, and additional features such as power windows and locks before making a purchasing decision. The same is true for a database.

Among the considerations for customers considering making a database purchase are:

- Performance
- Cost
- Number of platforms supported
- Number of applications supported
- Vendor's understanding of customer's business
- Reliability
- Quality of support
- Ease of use

At any point in its history, Oracle has had strength in some of these areas and weakness in others compared with the competition. But Larry Ellison has a good understanding of all of the elements that a customer considers when he or she is making a database purchase decision. So, before Larry launches an offensive against a competitor, he selects among the features and promotes only those elements where he knows that Oracle will win. All Oracle weaknesses are ignored. All strengths are emphasized, and as the fight evolves and Oracle or a competitor gains strength in an area, Larry resets the terms of the conflict so that they again favor Oracle.

This may be interpreted as classic product positioning, but it's more than that. The lesson to be learned is that business climates change rapidly, and Larry has succeeded, in part, because he willing to position and reposition the company and its products to meet changing competitive challenges. Instead of carving its positioning in stone, Oracle frequently changes course, always to the benefit of the company.

An interesting example is Oracle's positioning against competitor Ingres in the 1980s. The initial positioning was set in 1986, and the conflict had three main phases with each phase lasting approximately two years.

In the beginning, Oracle claimed to have a better implementation of the SQL language, based on industry luminaries E.F. Codd and Chris Date's commandments of relational technology. These commandments defined perfection in a relational database. Each was difficult to implement, and no vendor's implementation was anywhere near complete. Some of the elements Oracle did well and some of the elements Ingres did well. The game during this phase of the conflict was to convince the world that Oracle did as many of the commandments as possible, so Oracle took out advertisements that showed a grid with the elements on one axis and Oracle and Ingres on the other axis. Oracle took as liberal an interpretation of the commandments as it could when deciding whether they were met by Oracle and, of course, as conservative a bent as possible in deciding whether Ingres met them.

As Ingres came close to implementing all of Codd and Date's commandments ahead of Oracle, it was time for Oracle change the criteria on which the two companies would be compared. Larry looked at the two products and realized that one of the things that Ingres had sacrificed in the completeness of its implementation was performance. Though less complete, Oracle was faster. Therefore, the focus of this phase of the conflict was Oracle's outperformance of its competitors. Suddenly, the advertising grids that had contained compliance with the commandments were replaced with grids of benchmarks comparing Oracle and Ingres on different machines, showing the numbers for those environments where Oracle was much faster. The development teams at both companies, which had been scrambling to make their implementation compatible with the specification from Codd and Date, now refocused efforts on building their databases for speed.

Once Ingres started to catch up in terms of performance, Oracle changed the terrain again. This time, Larry changed the focus to the number of platforms on which the database was available. Ingres had been able to effectively optimize its offering because it only had a small number of platforms to consider. Oracle shifted this to its advantage and the advertisements that previously showed benchmark numbers were replaced with lists of computers that ran Oracle software but did not run Ingres. With the terrain reset once again, Ingres was forced into a situation where it had to react to Oracle. Knowing that Oracle had been working on its porting infrastructure for years, Ingres had to develop a strategy in response for how to make its database run on a wider range of computers.

This last phase was really the last chapter in the Oracle/Ingres conflict. The combination of a number of factors, including having to figure out how to make its offering more portable, finally began to wear on Ingres. It took a several years to play out, but at this point the Ingres story was over. Larry had shown brilliance in his maneuvering of the issues against Ingres as with other competitors. Some at Oracle claim that it is his interest in Japanese culture and his study of the samurai warrior that help him change the battle so adroitly to his advantage. I believe that it is more direct, that he fundamentally knows all of the parameters on which database software products will be compared. He then simply chooses the ones where he knows he will be able to win.

Deploy the Advertising Weapon

Oracle is famous for its aggressive advertising. The kind of advertising that Oracle, and specifically Larry Ellison, uses is very focused, targeted at a competitor or designed to make the phones ring at salespeople's desks.

To date, Oracle has not invested heavily in the promotion of the Oracle brand. Instead, it has relied on advertisements that will generate near-term tangible results. When asked about Larry's approach to advertising, Oracle's first advertising manager told me, "Advertising was a step beyond PR. Larry could say what he wanted and know that what was printed would be exactly what he had said. He did not have to rely on any kind of interpretation from a reporter."

Every ad that Oracle has ever run has been reviewed (and probably rewritten) by Larry Ellison.

Oracle's use of advertising as an implement of war started very early in the company's life. In 1986, Larry was faced with the realization that eventually the database market would stabilize, and when it did, the company with the most market share would win. More databases sold would enable more application sales, more services, and more databases. It was time to make aggressive moves to own the market, and Oracle was quick to use advertising as one of its weapons. That year, Oracle had only $120M in revenue, but it spent an astronomical $10M of that money on advertising.

With $10M in his arsenal, Oracle's first advertising manager told me, "We were able to cover all of the top technical trade publications. Because we were spending that kind of money, we were able to negotiate proper positioning. We always wanted to be up front in the book. We always wanted to be on the right hand page. We wanted all the premium positioning, and we didn't want to pay for it. But all of the magazines always caved because we were such an aggressive advertiser. They wanted to be able to point to us and say, 'look at what Oracle is doing and look at how successful they are.'"

Even though Ingres had better software technology than Oracle at that time, Oracle used advertising power to compare itself with Ingres—on Oracle's terms. Featuring the comparisons and benchmark numbers previously discussed, Larry used advertising to his advantage. They were Oracle's forum, and in the case of Ingres, as the head of advertising put it, "Larry would not be outlied by a bunch of professors from Berkeley."

Oracle also used advertising to hit other competitors, including DEC and HP, and he did it on the competitor's own turf. "We would deal with them directly, head to head, in the HP magazines—*HP World*—and the Digital magazines—*Digital News* and *Digital Review*," remembers the head of advertising. And Oracle's ads were in-your-face, claiming that the competitive products didn't do this, they didn't do that, and often asked "Why are you betting your career on products like that?"

In 1988, when Oracle entered the PC market with an implementation of Oracle for MS-DOS, the incumbent was Ashton-Tate, offering its dBase product. When Oracle announced its PC-based product, Oracle ran the famous triplane ad. It was direct, graphic, and according to the advertising manager at the time, "It was really the perfect thing because it forced Ashton-Tate into a defensive mode." At the time, Ashton-Tate virtually owned the PC database market and had done a lot of research which indicated that a relational database on the desktop was not important and was too complex for their users. "The triplane ad caused Ashton-Tate to take its eye off the ball. On the desktop, if they had stayed in that market, the company would have been just fine. Yet, it put all of its development resources into developing dBase IV, which was relational. We literally pushed them into a corner that they had to fight their way out of and they blew it. They totally responded to that aggressive form of marketing."

A couple of years after that, to demonstrate Oracle's industry dominance, the company ran an advertisement showing a pie chart of market shares in the database industry. The ad's original draft showed Sybase as having 8 percent of the market, with Oracle claiming more than five times that. When Larry reviewed the ad, he couldn't bear to give his then-target, Sybase, any credit at all and demanded that the ad be redesigned with Sybase lumped into the "Other" category, so that its name wouldn't even appear.

Throughout its history, most of Oracle's advertisements have been confrontational and employ a device one Oracle marketing person calls "Functional Marketing." Functional marketing is not necessarily pretty, it is about feature-and-benefit check boxes and performance numbers. Whenever Oracle was in a competitive position, which describes most of the history of the company, Larry would always demand comparative advertisements. One of the marketing people explained that it's, "like boxers before a fight, where they publish reach, height, weight, and age; Oracle ads feature comparisons similar to the boxer's statistics in a box-type comparison format." This analogy is a good one, as Oracle approached every competitor like a fighter, always ready to jump into the next ring.

Oracle's advertising format was very effective in per-suading customers and setting the Oracle agenda. The advertising manager told me, "Back then, we did a focus group and we asked people, 'What do you look at?'

'Well, we look at the magazines.' First they see the ads, then they see the articles. If they see these comparison charts in the ads, it really helps them set the criteria easily."

Many people assume customers do not read detail in an advertisement, but in the technical arena this is not true. The ad manager told me, "It is incredible what these people read. Particularly in the UNIX marketplace. Down at the very bottom where all of the copyright stuff goes, Rick Bennett put 'TRBA,' followed by the copyright sign. At least a half dozen people a week would call the direct marketing group and ask what the TRBA stood for. People really read this stuff and paid attention to it." (By the way, TRBA stands for The Rick Bennett Agency.)

Aggressive ads were not Oracle's only ingredient in turning competitive situations into sales. The company also had good tracking software, based on its own database, so that Oracle could place an ad and watch calls from it spike and then trail off on a daily or hourly basis. Based on the statistics, the design firm would do something as simple as change the background color of an ad and watch it spike again. Oracle tracked all of the direct marketing statistics closely so the advertising designers knew what was working and what was not working. The information that the designers got was from OASIS, Oracle's sales force automation application, where the calls that the advertisements generated were logged. This way, both designers and salespeople could quickly act on the data entered into OASIS, sometimes even generating a sale from a prospect proactive enough to call based on information in an ad.

On the advertising front, no tactic is too aggressive for Oracle. In the late 1980s, Oracle was granted free advertising space for twenty-four hours on a "traveling billboard." At the time, Informix had placed a competitive Oracle advertisement and Oracle responded by blowing up an advertisement and putting it on the traveling billboard where the text read: "Gentlemen, start your snails." The graphic showed benchmark numbers for Oracle in red and showed the lesser competitive benchmarks as snail trails, using a snail to denote each competitor. Oracle parked the traveling billboard in the Informix parking lot. I was told that this action caused Informix to retaliate by buying a fixed billboard located 1,000 feet from the Oracle headquarters building on Highway 101 in Redwood City, where Informix has run a series of inflammatory advertisements against Oracle ever since.

Lock Customers In and Competitors Out

Technology has certainly been a factor in Oracle's dramatic success, but the most powerful key that Oracle used to lock out the competition was not a technical one. The complex architecture and well-designed implementation of Oracle's database only works to Oracle's advantage in terms of keeping competitors out of accounts in the first place. The secret to locking in a customer for life lies in the issues associated with switching away from Oracle products once they are in use in a customer enterprise.

Keep competitors out: Product implementation barrier

Any potential competitor looking at the details associated with implementing a relational database quickly realizes that Oracle has built a tremendous barrier to entry. The Oracle database is a very large piece of software with complexity at every level.

A few of the technical elements Oracle thought through that make it hard for a competitor to consider improving on the implementation are:

- Portability that allows the core software to be moved to new computers easily
- Sophisticated logic that gracefully handles failures in the computer hardware or software
- Special software that allows Oracle to reap the performance advantage of advancements in disk drive, processor, and memory technology
- Network software that allows an Oracle database to be spread across multiple, even different, computers

These days, being in the business of building a relational database that can stand up to millions of transactions a day and run on a huge range of computers is like being in the Space Shuttle business. Anyone who wants to can compete with Boeing for the Space Shuttle business. Anyone, that is, with thousands of people, hundreds of millions of dollars, and a great deal of experience and expertise. Oracle has set the barrier to entry high enough that it is unlikely that the market will see a new viable competitor.

Keep customers in: Product switching barrier

Certainly the most significant barrier that Oracle built against its competition was the issue of a customer's switching cost to move from an Oracle database once a customer's data is in it. It was universally believed inside Oracle that "If you own the data, you own the customer." Oracle makes it easy to load information into an Oracle database from other (even older) database products. However, once a customer's information is stored in an Oracle database, the cost to a customer is very high to move that information over to another vendor's database.

The issues associated with switching include:

- The cost of buying a competitive product
- The cost of transferring the information into a competitive product
- The cost of learning the competitive product
- The cost of building the applications again using the competitive product
- The admission by the team of people who selected Oracle that they made a wrong decision

In addition to understanding a customer's predisposition not to switch from Oracle, the company also invented products and services to draw customers in. Anything that made it easy for customers to start using Oracle also made it hard for them to stop:

- Oracle built the SQL*Loader product, which would import data from competitive offerings into Oracle.
- Oracle consultants are highly trained in data conversion from other sources into Oracle.
- Oracle does not offer products that help customers export data from Oracle to some other database.
- Oracle does not publish the internal structure of an Oracle database, making it hard for a competitor to create software that takes data out of Oracle and puts it into another database.

Oracle has found it relatively easy to lock in a customer (and the ongoing revenue associated with that customer), while at the same time locking out the competition. While it may appear that this is a fortuitous by-product of developing a sophisticated product, it is not. Locking in a customer is a deliberate strategy at Oracle, a policy that has enabled the company to obtain and keep its market-leading position.

In looking at competitive entry barriers, most organizations look at the effort required to build a competitive product. These are usually technical or production barriers associated with a set of functions and the time and expertise required to build them. While this is useful in figuring out how to keep the competition out, Oracle has shown the world that it is only part of the story. Understanding the issues that will keep existing customers committed to your product—and your company—exposes a path for how to build a barrier to competitive entry, one that can last for generations of your product.

CHAPTER EIGHT

Talent

IN ANY FIELD, IT IS IMPORTANT TO HIRE THE BEST TALENT YOU CAN FIND FOR A PARTICULAR JOB. And that talent comes in all shapes, forms, and intelligence levels. Like the military, Oracle is only looking to recruit a few good men and women. Unlike the military, Oracle has a very targeted approach to its efforts.

What makes Oracle unique in this area is its method of attracting and employing high-caliber individuals. Oracle understands exactly what it takes to attract the individuals it targets and uses appealing techniques, such as confident interviews and attractive compensation packages, to get them to sign up. Once these individuals are "chosen" to work at Oracle, the company employs methods such as "Boot Camp" to indoctrinate them.

While some of the following recruiting tactics are universal, some are not. What is important is focusing your efforts to hire the talent your company needs—and wants— and then helping your recruits clearly understand the roles they are to play in the organization.

Recruit Athletes

Oracle targets intelligent individuals, and the company's personnel recruitment philosophy is simple: "Hire the athlete."

In comparing two candidates, Oracle will always seek out the candidate with the most potential, the most mental horsepower. The company does this practically to the exclusion of relevant industry experience.

In search of the "Athlete," Oracle recruits new college graduates aggressively from a list made up of only the top colleges in the country—and these recruits are not just computer science majors. Oracle recruits engineering, biology, chemistry, and math majors from the following colleges that make up "The List:"

- Brown
- UC Berkeley
- CalTech
- Carnegie-Mellon
- Harvard
- MIT
- Stanford

The theory is simple. If Oracle can find a smart person, it can teach that person to do whatever the company needs to get done. Oracle lets the schools do much of the legwork. For example, at college campuses, Oracle candidates have already been sorted by intelligence and personality, so the company can expedite the hiring process. What Oracle is looking for is a person who will bring a different perspective to the job, particularly if that person's education was in mathematics or chemistry, rather than computer science. Long term, the company believes that these individuals will be more valuable than someone with industry experience because they will have proven themselves to be both intelligent and versatile.

Oracle definitely has an employee profile and the company's pursuit of the types of candidates it wants to hire is effective. The reason: Oracle understands the kind of heady treatment that appeals to a bright, young, aggressive college student.

When I was an undergraduate at Harvard, I signed up for a number of scheduled corporate recruiter interviews, among them Oracle. I showed up for my Oracle interview ready to answer questions about relational database structure, the size of the relational database market—all of the things that you would expect to get asked in such an interview. Then, I walked into the empty interview cube where the head of Oracle recruiting was sitting with no papers or briefcase. He said, "Hello, Stuart. I want you to work at Oracle. We'll fly you to California whenever you want. Do you have any questions?" The interview was over in fewer than three minutes. I was sold. Any company that aggressive and confident was a place where I wanted to work.

My experience was not uncommon. A senior at Carnegie-Mellon University attending a college-sponsored job fair was approached by one of the Oracle recruiters. The recruiter was a former classmate he knew who had graduated the year before from the same institution. The Oracle recruiter said, "Hey, you've got to talk with this guy! He's really smart." The head of recruiting wasted no time, asking the student when he could come and visit Oracle. That was the interview.

A developer who started at Oracle the same time that I did said, "After the interview, I was left with a feeling that this is someone speaking my language; Let's skip all of the BS, we both know that I'm smart." When Oracle flew him out to California to interview, the recruiters put him up in a premium hotel, rented him a car, and paid all of his expenses. Already sold by the reception he had enjoyed from the company, he said, "My offer was high, higher than it needed to be, and it included stock. Joining Oracle was one of the easiest decisions I've ever had to make!"

Once Oracle has a recruit interested, the company sets a financial bar that meets or exceeds expectations. I remember in 1988, in an environment where my classmates were getting high-end offers of $28,000–$32,000 a year to be consultants for Bain and McKinsey, Oracle offered a seemingly staggering $35,000 a year. Oracle made me feel like it really believed in me. How could I possibly refuse?

Besides that, half of my graduating class—from the computer science department—was going to work at Oracle, too. In an interview with one of my classmates, the head of recruiting asked how many graduates there would be from the computer science department that year. My friend told him that there would be about thirty. The head of recruiting was unhappy. "We need 60," he complained, "We'll hire them all and we'll need more."

Oracle has hiring its target employee down to somewhat of a science. A vice president who brought more than a hundred people into Oracle explained to me that you look for four things:

Intelligence

This characteristic is easy to quantify because Oracle measures intelligence by GPA and college entrance board scores.

Compulsiveness

Oracle looks for a high degree of compulsiveness in prospective job applicants. The high-growth nature of the company requires a manager to have people who are so demanding of themselves that they simply have to get the job done, and get it done right.

Communicativeness

People who are highly communicative easily share their bright ideas with others and, as a result, can attack new problems and move into new areas of the company. In contrast, people who are not communicative are often relegated to working only in a single area because even if they have a great new idea, they may not be able to get the organization to understand and rally behind it.

Sense of Humor

Once it identified someone with the first three characteristics, Oracle looked for a person with a sense of humor. The reason: Humor tempers the first three to the point where an employee's ego is at least bearable. Further, the company believes that someone with a sense of humor is less likely to crumple under the pressure that Oracle puts on a person.

Recruiter Larry Lynn maintains that in ten minutes or less he can determine if a candidate meets the Oracle profile. And if he decided that a candidate was an Oracle "Athlete" and the candidate got to Oracle headquarters, there was a 90 percent chance that person would get an offer somewhere in the company. With that philosophy in mind, it is easy to see how Oracle is able to streamline the recruiting process and turn it into an efficient, productive machine.

When you find athletes, hire them!

Once Oracle identifies someone it considers to be Oracle material, the company makes sure that it hires that person. A woman who worked in Oracle's human resources department told me that the secret to getting a candidate to agree to an offer is figuring out what is really important to that person and getting it for him or her. When Oracle wanted to hire a candidate who was concerned about moving away from his family on the East Coast, the company offered to pay his long distance bills for two years. He accepted. When Oracle found a candidate who didn't want to move to California without his significant other, the company interviewed his significant other, hired them both, and moved them to California.

Early on, Oracle's hiring process was focused simply on bringing the brightest people into the company. Many people were hired without a specific position in mind. Oracle knew that by the time the recruits graduated and went through training, the company would have specific needs for them. Even nontechnical people who were bright and wanted to join Oracle were hired. These recruits generally took an entry-level position while they learned about the company and the technology. Some of the receptionists at Oracle's first campus were Stanford graduates, answering telephones just to get into the company. They went on to take other jobs in the company once they spent time learning about relational database technology and Oracle's personality.

The downside to Oracle's formula is clear. The company likely misses some fantastic candidates who may not have gone to an Oracle "approved" school. Since these potential employees go into the standard applicant pool, Oracle could easily not hire them. However, even though the company misses a huge number of people as a result of its policy, Oracle knows that it always gets a good success rate from "The List."

Another aspect of Oracle hiring that is somewhat counterintuitive is that the company encourages managers to hire people who are at least as good as they are or better. With the company growing fast, those people could take their manager's place as the manager moved up to take on new responsibilities. A side effect of this policy is that once engaged, it is self-perpetuating. It encourages managers to bring in college friends from the class below them and to apply the same strict criteria to incoming managers that was applied to them. It sets a clear standard to measure any job candidate against and enables a quick and defensible decision for every one.

Oracle's "Hire the Athlete" policy is enforced at the highest level of the company, with all offer letters signed personally by Larry Ellison. During my tenure, I sent more than twenty offer letters to Larry's desk for approval. Without fail, the ones without the right educational pedigree (or some other marking of native intelligence) got rejected and the ones with such evidence were approved in a hurry.

In one case, the concept of "Hiring the Athlete" was taken quite literally. When Oracle opened a search for Chief Legal Counsel, a large number of excellent candidates applied. One candidate was training for the Olympic luge event at the time he interviewed at Oracle. Many of the interviewers felt that the Olympic effort would distract the candidate from his prospective duties at Oracle and looked to other candidates. Larry Ellison felt exactly the opposite, that any person driven enough to make run at the Olympics would make a fantastic Chief Counsel. Not only did Oracle hire the athlete, Oracle supported his Olympic effort.

I hired a lot of people at Oracle, and the thought that sticks with me most strongly came from my first manager:

A people hire A people
B people hire C people

When employees decide to leave, Oracle does not worry too much about them. Those who depart after two or three years have put in a lot of time on behalf of the company and most still prove valuable to Oracle. In the last fifteen years, the company has seen a large number of ex-employees go out into the industry with Oracle knowledge. These same people have brought Oracle products into the departments of their new companies. They have also started new companies and built new products on top of the Oracle database. And after time away, some of them even return to Oracle wiser and full of new, exciting ideas for the company.

Indoctrinate with Company Culture

Many companies prefer—for fiscal or workload needs—to hire employees with experience so that they can begin working right away. Oracle is not one of these companies. Oracle prefers to hire individuals with the aptitude to learn and provides them with on the job culture and product training, which begins in "Boot Camp."

Although Oracle's indoctrination method requires extra time and money, the company yields real results, including a focus on employee teamwork, a sense of community, and a high level of employee loyalty, something not often found in work environments today.

Based on its hiring philosophy, Oracle ends up with scores of recent college graduates arriving every summer with no:

- Work experience
- Understanding of database technology
- Appreciation for Oracle's personality
- Actual computer experience (or in some case, very little)
- Kids
- Local friends
- House
- Spouse
- Favorite restaurant
- Commitments
- Life at all, basically

To speed integration into Oracle, the company puts every new employee into a three-week training program, which is referred to as "Boot Camp." A Boot Camp class consists of roughly thirty new hires headed into all different areas of the company. A future salesperson will be seated next to a developer or a human resources person. Throughout "Camp," the entire group is sequestered in a hotel, in classes from 8:00 A.M. to 6:00 P.M. during the week. On the nights and weekends, there are either mandatory events or assignments that need to be completed, so the experience is one of total immersion. While most of the presentations are technical in nature and there is a terminal at every desk, Boot Camp is much more about understanding Oracle's culture than learning a computer program. Every person speaking in front of or administrating the class is selected because he or she embodies some element of the Oracle Edge.

Before I started class, I met one of the people responsible for organizing it and one of the people who most embodies Oracle style. She is the ambassador to new hires and had been with Oracle since the early days, spending time as Larry Ellison's assistant. She was always well dressed, always organized, and put a personal element into every aspect of the class. She was our class "Den Mother."

Though not much older than we were, she referred to us as "her kids," and she personally went to the Price Club to get the huge quantities of soda and candy necessary to keep the group fueled. When it came time for anyone in the class to handle any of the elements of relocating to the Bay Area and starting a new job, she was quick with a name of a realtor, a description of a particular manager, or a recommendation for a good restaurant. Before starting class, we were being molded into optimal Oracle employees. And we were being watched. Everything at Boot Camp was competitive. The students divided into teams to create a product using Oracle technology. Each team had to present the product and the best team was rewarded. Outside of the classroom, we spent a day at a "Ropes Course" where we scaled walls and trees proving that we could work together.

A product manager friend of mine who had been through Boot Camp explained, "Oracle takes advantage of that impressionable stage. It's like when a chick hatches, the first thing it sees is its Mom. For us in the class, Oracle was mom. I measure every job I have had since Oracle against Oracle. The company gains amazing loyalty by forming young professionals in the Oracle style." Another graduate of Oracle Boot Camp told me that he felt, "Oracle succeeded in creating a network of people so that you could manage the work world."

Although Boot Camp's classroom experience is valuable, many of the benefits of Boot Camp are intangible. I found it incredibly useful to have friends in different departments within the company. It gave me a perspective of what was going on in the rest of the organization and people to call when I needed a favor.

Later, as a manager in the Desktop Group, I tried to have team outings on a regular basis that encouraged the type of intergroup interaction that we all experienced at Boot Camp. Sometimes, our group would challenge a group we worked closely with to an event as a way of getting some time together outside of the office. We played soccer against another product line and volleyball against the development team. At one point, we challenged the Desktop Support Group to a match, and in an effort to find a sport that no one knew how to play, we all agreed on broomball.

Broomball is like hockey, except sticks are replaced with brooms and the puck is replaced with a playground ball. The event is held in a gym. I volunteered to reserve the gym for our event. Unfortunately, when I called the fitness center to reserve a time, the staff there was not helpful. "I'm sorry, the gym cannot be reserved by a group at any time," I was told, despite the fact that basketball and volleyball events peppered the calendar. Not to be deterred, I asked to speak with the staff person's manager. "I'm not sure you want to do that," the fitness center administrator continued, "Our manager is very strict and I'm sure she will not be willing to make any exceptions for you, even if she is willing to talk with you." Concerned that my broomball game was going to be cancelled, I asked, "Who is your manager?" When he responded with the name, I'm only glad the fitness center administrator couldn't see the smile on my face. She had been in Boot Camp with me and was someone whom I could certainly call for a favor. Broomball was going to happen after all.

Having a class that included people from a variety of departments had another advantage. Current Oracle employees, despite their hectic schedules, were called upon to teach the classes. In many companies, existing employees would resist the responsibility of teaching new recruits or they would simply not put much effort behind it. But faced with teaching a class that included someone who would end up in your group gave existing employees incentive to be engaging, informative, and more exciting than the previous Boot Camp presenter.

The highlight of every Boot Camp is the visit from Larry Ellison. We were told at the beginning that there was a good chance that Larry would come to the class and talk with us. Though normal attire for the class was casual, we were instructed that, at any time, class could be stopped and we would have fifteen minutes to put on suits, ties, and skirts. This event was called an "LJE Alert." After two false alarms, Larry did come visit our class, and we all looked our best. His visit, although brief, was very inspiring because it told each one of us in that room that we were important to Oracle.

The Oracle Boot Camp experience was complete. When the formal training was through, the company held a party at the entrance to corporate headquarters. There was a tent immediately outside of the front door to welcome us to our new home. There was food and alcohol, and current Oracle employees greeted us to share war stories about the rigors of Boot Camp. The bonding process was well under way.

While some of the benefits of Oracle Boot Camp are intangible, some are very tangible. Young Oracle employees work long hours—often fifteen to eighteen a day. Although not always physically at their desks, they are with other Oracle people nearly every waking minute of every day, devoting mental energy to Oracle. When they ski during the weekend, they talk about Oracle on the lift. When they go out to dinner, they discuss competitive products before ordering an appetizer. They go to parties hosted by Oracle people and attended by Oracle people who talk about Oracle. The way Oracle captures the energy and dedication of young talent is powerful and provides long-term benefits to the company.

I estimate that the open-mindedness, creativity, and bonding experience that Oracle promotes among new hires in Boot Camp saves the company six months of on-the-job orientation, product teaching, and employee training activities. It also sets an expectation for how Oracle employees will be consumed by their positions at the company.

I suppose that I am a textbook example of how well the Oracle process of indoctrination worked. Two of my camp classmates ended up being my roommates and by the end of class, having been taught to live like Oracle people, we found a sprawling house in Hillsborough (one of the wealthiest towns in California) to rent. I still keep in touch with more than half of my classmates from Boot Camp, most of whom are no longer at Oracle. But, when we get together, we still talk about Oracle.

While it is almost impossible to buy employee loyalty, companies that offer a chance for individuals to bond during their first week(s) are on the right track. When everyone is new, no question is too dumb, no response too naïve, and no activity too silly. Although many companies cannot afford to go to the extent that Oracle does to indoctrinate employees, the experience gained during this type of process allows employees to feel more comfortable with each other, with your products, and with your company in general. When employees understand—and actually meet—their resources, they feel empowered. And the result is most often to the benefit of the entire organization.

Communicate Your "Mantra"

There are several fundamental guidelines that separate Oracle from the rest of the business pack. They are written in the Oracle "Mantra," a set of guidelines that describe how Oracle runs itself and how it drives its unique personality, both of which translate directly into its success. The guidelines, which permeate the entire company, from Larry Ellison to the most junior assistant, help to communicate a corporate ideology.

When I was at Oracle, the Mantra consisted of the letters P, C, C. Any person who worked at the company when I did will tell you that letters define the Oracle product tenets of:

Portability—the database is designed to run on any hardware platform

Compatibility—works with industry standards

Connectability—the database is designed to be distributed across any network

While they may not be appropriate for your organization, these simple letters set a fierce development direction for Oracle. Determining how to implement a particular feature, junior developers already know their choice, at a minimum, needs to have these attributes. In deciding the direction for future releases of the core database, the senior architects already know how their decisions will be judged.

One of the greatest distractions at Oracle is figuring out how to work with products and technologies that are platform specific, meaning they only support one type of product or configuration of products. For example, many computers have software extensions that are platform specific, so they can enhance applications that are used only on that particular platform. Looking at the problem with the Oracle Mantra in mind makes decisions dealing with platform-specific attributes easy.

In 1991, Microsoft began promoting its OLE (Object Linking and Embedding) technology to developers building applications for the Windows platform. The technology had some very strong technical merit. It enabled one application to intelligently communicate with another application. Therefore, if this technology was used by both applications, a Microsoft Word user could put an Oracle database report into a Microsoft Word document. Then, when the data changed in the Oracle database, the data would automatically be updated in the Microsoft Word document.

At first glance, OLE support looked like a feature that would be important to have in an Oracle database report generator. But deeper investigation showed that supporting OLE on the Windows platform would require structural changes to Oracle technology that would not be portable to other platforms. Because OLE only exists on Windows, and not on all of the other platforms that Oracle supports, to make structural changes to support it would violate the tenet of Portability. The decision not to support OLE with Oracle's core products, as seductive as the prospect initially seemed, was easy to make. The Mantra set a clear direction.

Businesses of all kinds can benefit from a mantra. To clearly communicate your corporate ideology, figure out what product or service characteristics will differentiate your organization and translate those into simple words. Then, publish the words and meanings—in annual reports, corporate presentations, on the Web site, and around the company.

One of the people who started Oracle at the same time that I did told me, "To be useful, the vision has to be communicated in a sentence, not in a five-page e-mail."

I suggest giving employees simple words to define what they should do. But be sure to choose these words carefully because you will be amazed at how quickly they are adopted and become part of the corporate dialect.

CHAPTER NINE

Management Philosophy

ONCE A COMPANY RECRUITS THE TALENT IT WANTS—AND NEEDS—IT IS IMPORTANT FOR EMPLOYEES TO UNDERSTAND THE ORGANIZATION'S MANAGEMENT PHILOSOPHY. At all levels, Oracle has employed effective management tactics to help its employees understand the value of teamwork and how to create personal opportunity in a changing, often reorganizing, environment.

Throughout its history, across the company Oracle has created a very competitive environment. Not only has the organization been fiercely competitive against other database software providers, but it has always been quick to challenge its own employees. Oracle's first head of support told me, "Oracle taught me how to win."

Just knowing what management expects can help many employees to achieve beyond what they could have imagined.

Teach People How to Win

One of the best examples of Oracle challenging its employees came in 1988 when the company was besieged with quality problems and customer complaints. Larry

Ellison threw down a gauntlet for the support organization. The challenge was to win the Dataquest (an independent industry analyst organization) award for the best customer service in the database industry.

The odds against Oracle winning seemed pretty high, given that at the time the company was focused on growing revenues and market share with the attention to customer care and quality falling much lower on the list. Faced with the challenge, the Oracle Support Group added people and upgraded its infrastructure so that it could track calls, problems, and bugs on-line. The group set very aggressive customer service metrics that measured how long it took to answer the phone, how long it took to call a customer back, and how long it took to resolve a problem.

When Oracle Support won Dataquest's award, Larry was so incredulous that he wouldn't talk about it or publish it for three months. He just couldn't believe it. When it became clear that the award was legitimate, Larry heaped on the recognition. He personally showed up to Support meetings, just to meet the team and to answer questions. Larry also paid for the Support Group to spend a lavish weekend in Monterey, complete with a big dinner and party at the Aquarium. At the event, every Support person received a sweatshirt decorated with brightly colored fish to recognize the accomplishment. Though that was ten years ago, you can still see tattered versions of these sweatshirts on senior Support staff during a casual Friday at Oracle.

Setting down a big challenge for a team and richly recognizing team members when they accomplish it is one of the best motivators in any organization.

Give Power to Individuals and Teams

Oracle gives people at every level the kind of autonomy they need to be able to succeed or fail in their jobs. When I asked a former group product manager what her favorite part of being at Oracle was, she explained, "A lot of people have to wait until they are 35–40 years old to get responsibility where the results will impact the bottom line. I was fortunate enough to get that kind of responsibility at age 22. Of course at the time, it was a little scary."

She described her first six months at Oracle as "dealing with ambiguity and pandemonium." But once she got acclimated, she figured out how to make order of the craziness. She got to choose how she would handle customers, product releases, and developers, and she built the processes around her. The organization wanted her to create more than just products, and that set her up on an accelerated track. She hired her first direct report less than a year later and took a leadership role in creating a whole new product team. "Oracle didn't shelter me," she reflects, "Oracle prepared me for what the real world is about. The real world is about figuring out how to excel in an environment where there is no structure—how to build order from nothing."

One of the assumptions of this autonomy strategy is employees with high intelligence and a strong desire to succeed. Another is that there are responsible managers making sure that none of their charges is in over his or her head. With this as a foundation, Oracle gives its employees room to excel.

A developer in the core group told me, "What makes Oracle fun is that you don't show up to work the first day as the low person on the totem pole—a slave to your master.

You have a lot of autonomy. But even though you have a lot of power, your manager has even more power, so he or she could make a change without tiptoeing around a lot of process."

The Oracle environment is one where process falls secondary to output, giving people the freedom they need to get their job done. Another developer told me, "I got to Oracle just after it went public. I joined the tools group and I was one of just three people building SQL*Forms (one of Oracle's core front-end products). Within about six months, the team was six guys and I was the most senior person on the team. In hindsight, it blows me away! We could innovate where we wanted to without a lot of interference from higher up."

A vice president of development at Oracle makes sure that prospective employees understand the positives and the negatives of empowerment. Once he has established that he wants to hire a candidate, he tells them this:

It is OK to say "no" at Oracle.
We will load you up.
We will keep loading you up like a mule.
We will keep putting loads on your back and expect you to
    carry them.
If you never bray,
We will overload you.
You will sink to your knees;
You will fail.
But if you bray,
If you prioritize,
If you are not afraid to say "no,"
You will succeed.

With responsibility, Oracle creates opportunity. A woman who had come into Oracle from being a field sales representative at Data General told me, "As soon as I got to Oracle, I got to do a huge range of things with a high level of responsibility. I influenced product direction, set the marketing strategy for my area, went out and did sales calls, and took charge of several product launches. In all of my various jobs, I was never a person or two away from Larry Ellison. The opportunity and the visibility was incredible."

In my opinion, one of the reasons that Oracle hires a large number of employees with little or no prior work experience is because new hires don't know any better. They don't bring any preconceived ways of doing things to the job. New Oracle employees rarely say a task is impossible because they don't have the experience to know. As a result, they put creative minds to work on a problem and come up with an ingenious answer. "Oracle taught me how to own a problem, and that gives me the confidence to solve it." is something that I have heard from both current and past employees.

Sometimes a sense of empowerment comes directly from successfully dealing with disorganization. Oracle's yearly reorganization (discussed later in this chapter) comes at the same time that the new college hires are arriving, so more than a few recruits find that the job they were offered in April no longer exists in July. An associate product manager told me, "The day I started work, I was told that the job that I was hired for was gone. The manager of the division was gone. I panicked. But in the same breath, they told me that I had eight different jobs from which I could chose—effectively being able to create my own position. It was exhilarating, knowing that there was that much opportunity at Oracle and that I would have the freedom to select from it."

Most organizations benefit from letting individuals control their own destiny. And often there is no need to shield them from the disorganized elements of the company. When bright people see a problem and they feel like they have the support to impact it, they will solve it.

My favorite example of this comes from 1986, when the director of marketing came into a cubicle shared by two young marketing people and asked, "We have to do a magazine and a User Group. Who wants to do which?" They decided right there on the spot. Today, the User Group has tens of thousands of members with annual events worldwide, and the magazine boasts a circulation of 135,000.

Spend Money on what Matters

Employees in a large organization will always ask for more money and resources than are available. Even if a company has the money and/or resources, it should not always acquiesce to all of an employee's demands. Over the years, Oracle has done a good job of identifying and providing those items that will make the most difference to a particular employee.

For the sales people, the answer is simple. It's money. Oracle's sales compensation system has always been focused on richly rewarding successful salespeople. In development, the answer is equipment. Any engineer was able to get a leased line and equipment at home for a remote development setup if they asked for it. Of course, that meant that you were supposed to work at night, but that also indicated that Oracle knew that your work was important.

For new hires, the answer varied. Oracle offered new employees cash advances to buy cars or to get apartments. A developer who benefited from all this caretaking said, "From day one, you get a definite message of trust from Oracle."

Spending money that enables employees makes them productive. Oracle was actively trying to create an environment where employees could outperform their own expectations. Expense items that supported an employee were usually approved. In contrast, I rarely saw Oracle approve the use of a consultant or a contractor. The subtle line of distinction is drawn around the idea that Oracle wants its own employees to do the thinking about Oracle issues. Oracle believes that no one outside could deeply understand the considerations as well or could make as good a decision.

In general, most organizations can yield more work and loyalty from their employees by figuring out what they can provide that will make an employee's life better.

Make a Commitment; Keep It

In a fast-paced, growing organization, if you say you're going to do something, you had better do it! Oracle has set an expectation that a statement made about doing something is as good as a promise. I believe there are several ways Oracle fosters a strong sense of commitment among people inside of the company, including:

Respect

Oracle employees appreciate their own and others' intelligence, so there is a sense of respect that motivates people to make good on their commitments.

Competition

Most people who join Oracle are ambitious and competitive. They want to be sure that when the next reorganization comes, they will not have an unfulfilled promise outstanding that allows another employee to be better positioned for advancement.

Failure

Very few people who join Oracle have experienced failure. Many come directly from a successful experience at college and, idealistically, believe that not meeting a commitment is equivalent to failure.

A senior manager illustrated this simple "say what you mean and mean what you say" principle to me with this example. His manager was on Oracle's Management Committee, and at one of the committee's meetings his manager committed his team to taking responsibility for a series of competitive analysis papers written by the next meeting. Even though the order went out, by the next Management Committee meeting, the papers had not been completed. When the manager met with his staff, there was hell to pay. Although there were lots of perfectly valid reasons why the papers had not been done, all of which were out of the control of his staff, the manager didn't care. The important thing was the commitment. His team was authorized to do whatever it took to get the job done. They had failed. To make his point, when the next round of commitments came up, the manager made a list of the things to be done and required each member of his staff to sign his or her name next to the commitment. The impression was made. By the next meeting, all of the deliverables were met on time.

Think Like a Shareholder

One of the most illuminating conversations that I had at Oracle was with one of my fellow product managers. He always brought a calm and thoughtful approach to work, and on one particular day I was in need of a thoughtful approach, although I didn't yet know it. My manager set me to the tedious task of flipping through support documents so that we could determine the sales that our products had been involved in during that period. The undercurrent was a dispute with another business unit over revenue recognition.

When I told my colleague what I was up to, he asked, "Is what you are doing right?" I had been asked by my manager to do this so, "Of course, it was right," I told him. "Would the shareholders want you to do this?" he replied. Of course they wouldn't, I thought to myself. The shareholders would be angry that I was spending my time on anything not related to getting the next product out. And wait a minute, I'm a shareholder! He had a point. As a company, Oracle puts serious effort into getting employees to personally understand that they are owners of the company and, as such, should think like stockholders. Most employees are awarded company stock options, and virtually all participate in the lucrative employee stock purchase plan.

Fortunately for me, I managed to escape the task of counting pennies against the other group, but my approach to work was forever changed. Now, I challenge anyone working for me to take a personal stake in the company and I explain why. When employees know what they are doing can increase the value of their shares, more often than not, they work harder do the right thing on behalf of and for the company.

Be an Accessible Manager

Although Oracle is greatly influenced by its leader, many employees do not feel intimidated by Larry Ellison. The reason is because he, like most other Oracle managers, is accessible.

My first roommate was a developer working on new tools products for Oracle. Not long after he started, one of his coworkers was hired out of Oracle for an astronomical salary. Figuring that he was worth just as much, my roommate sent off a quick e-mail note directly to Larry Ellison asking for a raise and explaining why. Almost immediately, Larry responded, saying that he understood and that my roommate would be well taken care of in the next round of salary adjustments (which typically happened in the summer). Whether the raise ever materialized was not as important to my roommate, a twenty-one-year-old developer, than the fact that the president of the company had responded quickly and directly to his e-mail. In fact, the stunt earned my roommate a degree of personal notoriety with Larry, as Larry enjoyed it when employees were quick to present their accomplishments.

Another of my roommates, who was something of a prankster, worked on Oracle documentation. With his desktop publishing tools, he enjoyed spoofing current Oracle advertisements. Although my roommate had been at Oracle only a year, he was bold enough to poke fun at Oracle products, the Oracle data center, and even Larry in his versions of the print ads. Naturally, the parodies made their way to the presidential office. Fortunately, Larry found them humorous. And after an exchange of mail notes about the ads, my roommate sent Larry a mail note saying that he would like to do some real advertising for Oracle. Nothing happened immediately, but two years later, Larry told the head of the application tools group to take my roommate in as head of tools advertising. Larry thought that my roommate would be creative and had a sense of humor. Again, two years passed before Larry's hand reached down to my roommate again, inviting him to join Oracle's media server group because Larry wanted his creativity to build commerce applications for the media server.

One of Oracle's first finance people, who has been in a number of startups since she left Oracle, shows admiration for how available Larry is to employees. "In really good start-ups, the CEO is known by both the clients and the employees," she says.

In most organizations, however, getting direction from the top means skipping management processes, often at the risk of making people in between feel bad. The Oracle philosophy says that anyone with enough gumption to take an idea to the CEO's office deserves to live or die by that idea. Process then goes out the window.

Like Larry, all CEOs can benefit from staying in touch with employees. But, if they choose to short circuit the management chain, CEOs have to be fair about supporting good ideas and penalizing bad ones.

Spoil the Best Employees

When it comes to employees with good ideas, Oracle definitely plays favorites. These employees are richly rewarded, while others are overlooked or terminated.

When I worked under the first VP of development for the desktop group, he always claimed, "The Oracle bonus process is inherently arbitrary and unfair." While it may have served as a great line for diffusing complaints from people who felt they had been overlooked, his comment could not have been further from the truth. Oracle's bonus and raise process was designed specifically to reward top performers and to pass all others over. "Oracle is not a socialist company," my manager was told when his bonus and raise recommendations had been rejected. He had made the critical mistake of spreading his pool across too many people.

In my time as a manager awarding bonuses and raises, at least 10 percent of any group received zero raise and zero bonus. The majority of people got raises and bonuses below the average. And a few star employees received raises, bonuses, and stock packages that well exceeded their total annual compensation. Giving an employee no raise or bonus is Oracle's way of letting an individual know that it's time for a change. Giving an employee a large raise and bonus also sends a clear message and works as a great retention tool.

Oracle's bonus policy reinforces the concept of the highest common denominator. The idea is to motivate a star performer to set the standard. Every other employee will stretch his or her limits to achieve that standard as well. Instead of aiming at a standard that many employees can hit, the company sets Larry Ellison as the standard and highly compensates anyone who comes even close.

In practice, this policy works very effectively in the high-growth, highly competitive technology industry. Employees are aggressively recruited out of firms like Oracle and Oracle knows that there will be some attrition. Given that, the company knows that it cannot retain everyone, but it works hard to insure that it retains the truly exceptional employees. In any company, a selective raise and bonus policy can be effective at motivating star performers and providing a visible incentive to new hires.

Don't Be Afraid to Terminate

Many companies have elaborate processes that a manager has to go through in order to fire someone. Oracle managers only do what is required by the government in order to terminate an employee. Any company that hires as many people as Oracle does is bound to bring in some people who are not a good fit. Oracle may hire people who are inappropriate for the company, put someone into a job that is not right for them, or simply have a situation where two personalities do not work together.

In any case where there is tension, the situation can be bad for the employee, bad for the manager, and, most importantly, bad for the team. A person who is not right for a job often will:

- Demand too much from a manager
- Not get the job done
- Force the team to pick up the slack

One employee who is not right for a job can poison an entire group, which is why Oracle is prepared to act swiftly in the case of a bad fit. Before terminating an Oracle employee, a manager must determine whether the employee is wrong for his or her group or wrong for the company as a whole. Informal, but standard, policy within Oracle for an employee who is a bad fit for a job but is deemed useful elsewhere in the company is to give that employee thirty days to find a new position within the company.

Often, a manager will send the employee home while he or she is looking, so as not to affect the group further. Sending an employee home also sends the message that if he or she is not able to find something else within the company in thirty days, that employee is not welcome back at Oracle. If a manager does not want to see the employee transfer within the company, the manager lets his or her management and human resources know that the employee should be terminated and why. Provided that there is some compelling rationale, approvals come back quickly and the employee is given two weeks notice.

A vice president of engineering at Oracle told me simply, "We do a fast fail. Oracle's not for everybody." He explained that in engineering one of the occasional problems with new hires that he thought would fit is that they find themselves in need of more infrastructure, tighter bounds than Oracle imposes. When that happens, they come to him after a couple of months and say, "I'm sorry. I just can't get grounded. How do you people work?" Oracle requires employees to take initiative, to be able to see a whole project and how their piece fits in. But some people don't understand that and Oracle lets them go.

All new hires to Oracle are informed that their relationship with Oracle is "at will," meaning that either Oracle or the employee can terminate the relationship at their will. In fact, this is a needless formality, because California law supports "at will" employers, but I believe that Oracle lets employees know this specifically to set employee's expectations correctly.

While its termination policy may seem harsh, I believe that it is one of the factors that keeps Oracle fast paced and efficient. A development manager at Oracle told me, "When you have one person in the group who is not carrying his or her weight, it turns the group against that person." It is easy for a large organization to support deadwood—employees who aren't doing their jobs—but doing so drags down the expectation level for everyone in the organization. It lowers the bar in terms of employee motivation, expectations, and output. Oracle doesn't tolerate lowering the bar, nor should any organization.

Shake Up Your Organization

There is a long-standing joke at Oracle that goes like this: "If you don't like your manager, just wait a couple of months. It'll change." Every year, shortly after the close of the financial year at the end of May, Oracle reorganizes. I spent nearly seven years at Oracle, and in that time I had seven different titles and reported to twenty-two different managers.

Oracle's yearly reorganization impacts the sales, marketing, and product line organizations, but only rarely core development. The goals for a particular reorganization vary from focusing on market segments to focusing on product areas to creating exciting new opportunities for particular individuals. The issue of reorganization has its critics and its costs, but without it Oracle undeniably would not have been able to adjust to its rapidly changing marketplace.

On the positive side, the yearly reorganization:

Keeps people on their toes

In practice, the reorganization means that some large percentage (estimated at nearly 25 percent) of employees get a different position or a different manager in fewer than twelve months. In the face of that prospect, employees make it a point to take on more visible projects and to make sure that their accomplishments are understood by people throughout the management chain. The knowledge that your achievements will likely impact your situation in the foreseeable future encourages employees to take chances and excel.

Forces a yearly evaluation of people

Every company tells employees that managers provide at least yearly performance evaluations. When push comes to shove, however, in most companies the written employee evaluation slips to the bottom of the priority queue and rarely happens on time, if at all. At Oracle, every manager is forced to evaluate all of his or her people, at least informally, in order to decide upon those who will rise to the top with a promotion and those who are expendable and will get reassigned. While the manager may not actually fill out human resources forms, after a reorganization, all employees know clearly what their manager thought of their performance over the previous year.

Provides meaningful feedback on performance

In my time at Oracle, I never did receive a written evaluation of my job performance. What I did receive instead was a more tangible and important evaluation of my yearly performance: a promotion. As an employee, it was much more satisfying to receive the positive reinforcement of additional job responsibilities than a piece of paper with numbers rating my performance on a scale from one to five. And as a manager, it is nice to have a yearly event that forces the recognition of individual accomplishments.

Keeps life interesting

Most people come to Oracle to learn, to be challenged, and to get exposure to exciting new areas. One of the advantages of being employed at Oracle is the ability to move within a division or even to a completely different area of the company. The time to make that move is during the yearly reorganization, or perhaps just after it, as new managers rush to round out new organizations. While the idea of new and different challenges does not appeal to everyone, for the most part, it does to the people that Oracle proactively recruits.

Serves as a corporate version of "Rags to Riches"

In addition to personal challenges associated with yearly advancement comes compensation and stature. Oracle does not care about seniority or experience when it chooses which employee to put in a position and what to pay that individual. As a result, junior people can ascend to positions of great responsibility, stature, and salary. These success stories are visible to every Oracle employee and serve as significant inspiration to people at every level. Everyone at Oracle has a shot every year to advance, which is essentially the American Dream. A corporate icon, Larry Ellison proves it is possible to transform oneself from a man on the street to a billionaire. I believe that this equal advancement opportunity is the heart of personal motivation and the reason why many Oracle employees come to work in the morning.

Clearly, there are also negatives to shaking up an organization every year. The downsides that have impacted Oracle include:

Limited ongoing employee measures

Many jobs include tasks that require months or years to go by before their impact can be accurately measured. This is particularly true for programs that involve cooperation with partner companies where there can be a lot of organization, some development work, and then cross-training for the program to get off the ground. An example of this is Oracle's work with a new hardware platform partner. Someone at Oracle first recognizes that a new computer has a competitive advantage and that Oracle should run on it. Then, he or she forges a relationship with the manufacturer. Months pass as the Oracle software is adapted for the new system, and even more months pass as the industry is educated about the new product. In the meantime, the person who initiated the project has been reorganized into a different area of the company. If he or she was wrong about the platform, that employee will be in a new position by the time the facts are in and his or her ineptitude will be hidden. If the employee was right, he or she will probably not be appropriately recognized for a great accomplishment.

Loss of valuable process expertise

Systems involving Oracle software tend to be very complex and provide a wide range of opportunities for defects or bugs. A lot of experience is required to understand all of the things that can go wrong in a complete database system and to determine what needs to be tested in order to guarantee a solid product. When a developer goes to another project, there is no formal mechanism for that engineer to leave the critical information he or she has learned in the process to the next person. In essence, the secret recipe dies when that developer leaves and it needs to be recreated the next year.

Sacrifices in product quality

There is always an outstanding list of defects in Oracle products, and that list is divided by product group. For some products, it is easy to see the relationship between a long list of defects and a long string of reorganizations in a particular group. It could be due to a lack of accountability or insufficient time in a position to understand the product process, but this relationship is often drawn. Subsequently, the reorganization is blamed for sacrifices in product quality.

To say that yearly organizations work for the entire company is an overstatement. For example, the core technology team that writes the software that is the heart of an Oracle database does not undergo yearly reorganizations. Here there is great value in keeping deep system expertise, and the company cannot afford to have people relearn it on an annual basis.

For Oracle sales, support, marketing, and product lines, the yearly reorganization process has enabled the company to adjust to a rapidly changing marketplace while keeping the organization alive and demanding the best from individuals. On the whole, any company considering regular reorganizations should weigh the positive and negative factors in their marketplace before trying to implement this type of structured change.

See Opportunity in Change

Instead of being afraid of change, Oracle depends on it. The fact that Oracle has made its database software run on so many different computer platforms means that customers can choose Oracle and know they will be safe when the next "hot" computing platform comes along. With Oracle, they will have the opportunity to change when more compelling products are available.

The same is true inside of Oracle. Employees who perform know that they will be taken care of by the company. Oracle creates change to make sure that employees and the infrastructure are ready for it. The yearly reorganizations give people a time to reset, to think outside of their current job.

Even Larry Ellison embraces change. He is always ready to hear new ideas for how to expand Oracle's product set. As a result, Oracle is the only one of the database companies to venture into other product areas. For example, in 1986, Oracle initiated the Oracle Applications group to build high-level software that would take advantage of the Oracle database. In 1992, the company created the New Media Division to create products that deliver video to consumers. And in 1996, Oracle created NCI, the network computer company, to create technology for powerful, low-cost workstations.

So many companies perish or stagnate because they are afraid of change. They find something successful and they want to be able to keep doing it forever. What they ignore is that change is inevitable. If it is profitable, competitors will be attracted to a share of the profits. If it is not viable, their business will simply evaporate. The best response for any company, in any industry, is to anticipate change.

CHAPTER TEN

Surviving a "Crash"

L IKE MANY FAST-GROWING, SUCCESSFUL COM-
PANIES, ORACLE ENJOYED THE LIMELIGHT AND
ITS REPUTATION FOR EXCELLENCE. With Larry Ellison promoting the "grow at all costs" mentality, the company continued to hire what it considered to be only the best and
brightest individuals, pay its salespersons handsomely, and
push its product into Fortune 500 accounts.

Employees knew that Oracle was aggressive in every
aspect of its business, from sales to accounting. It was
understood that the optimistic policies and actions had put
the company on the map and made Oracle the market share
leader of relational databases.

Then, in 1990, Oracle hit the wall. In what seemed a
matter of days, earnings were low, products were late, and
the stock price plummeted from almost 30 to a low of 5 3/8.
The company was at the brink of insolvency. Those who
had been there a long time were in a state of denial. "How
could this have happened to the mighty Oracle?" But they
knew. Oracle had put in place some questionable strategies
under the "growth at all costs" doctrine and now the company would have to pay.

Identify Crucial Issues

An aggressive company, it is not surprising that many of Oracle's missteps were focused on making the company appear larger than it really was to the outside world. These included:

Booking revenue early

The nature of software sales—specifically database software sales—offers room for interpretation regarding when revenue can be truly counted or "booked." A typical database sale is composed of the database software, supporting applications, and on-site consulting to make those products work once they are installed. Therefore, the earliest revenue from the sale could be counted is when the invoice is presented to the customer. The latest is when all of the products have been delivered, the customizations have been made, and the system is running correctly. What Oracle used to its advantage was the time between those two points, which at the time was considered an accounting gray area. In the late 1980s, Oracle took the most optimistic route, booking revenues at the earliest point in time. As a result of this practice, Oracle was always a quarter ahead of itself in stating booked revenue, hoping that only a few, if any, of the current customers would return their Oracle products and ask for their money back. Provided that happened, and revenues the next quarter would be even stronger, the process could go on forever. If more customers returned software than the company expected or more customers couldn't pay their bills than the company expected, the company would be in trouble. If the next quarter's revenues didn't eclipse the previous ones, the company would also be in trouble. It was the combination of the these that caused the collapse in early 1990.

The fact that Oracle was accounting for revenue in this manner was public. Anyone adept at reading a corporate 10-K statement could have looked at Oracle's in 1989 and realized that Oracle was "laying down the track in front of a moving locomotive." But no one seemed to care. The auditors put their stamp on it, the stock was going through the ceiling—there was no end in sight. Simple denial is the only explanation for why anyone close to the company couldn't see The Crash coming.

Stuffing the channel

In order to show Wall Street analysts and other companies that Oracle was an industry leader, the company did what it could to show high unit volume shipment. To support this effort, Oracle sold database software products to distributors that, in turn, resold the database with their own consulting or applications. But, because Oracle was the industry leader, it could force a distributor to receive more copies of the software than it needed at the time. So, while Oracle claimed a certain number of units "sold," a significant number of those units were sitting on warehouse shelves at distributors. Oracle used this tactic with direct customers as well. In some instances, a customer was promised and even paid for an Oracle product that was still in development. Sometimes, the company even shipped incomplete or defective non-production versions of the product to the customer in order to claim shipment. In one case, although the product was not far enough along to ship in any form, Oracle wanted to book the revenue that quarter so (according to rumor) it expressed the customer a blank tape with the product label on it to claim shipment.

This practice was bound to end. With a limited number of resellers, a limited amount of space in their warehouses and a limited amount of patience on their part, the situation was not stable. When the company's stock crashed, this situation also came to a head.

Paying the price of the CAP

Oracle's innovative selling program, previously discussed as "the CAP," also enabled the company to claim it had sold product that it had yet to deliver because customers made commitments to buy Oracle products for multiple years. Remember, Oracle's customers heard: "If you buy databases for ten computers this year and promise to buy databases for fifty computers over the next five years, we'll give them all to you at the special rate that we have now. Prices are going up, it's the fourth quarter and we are ready to deal." Oracle, in turn, offered discounts approaching 80 percent, recognized or "booked" that revenue, and kept on selling. Now, Oracle had customers who required service but wouldn't generate any more revenue for at least other three or four years.

Without identifying these problems, Oracle couldn't have made the changes it needed to make to survive. In any turnaround situation, the first step is to make sure that you're solving the problems that will make a difference to your company's survival.

Turn the Company Around

Although Oracle had put itself in a tough financial position, the company was resilient. With Larry at the helm, the company quickly began to take steps to turn itself around. After the crash, in many ways, Oracle became a stronger company because the strategy it executed was focused on moving the company from a startup to a mature business. These tactics are good advice for any company that has grown quickly and perhaps gotten off track in the process.

Hire seasoned executives

Once these practices were exposed to the world, Oracle was no longer a startup. It had to act like a mature company quickly or perish. Larry went into seclusion for three days after the stock crashed. When he returned, he made critical decisions that put Oracle back on track and set its course for a bright future. Larry did this by recognizing that he had built a company around his vision of data management, but that the company had gotten too large for him to run by himself. Oracle needed seasoned, professional managers.

Soon thereafter, Larry hired Jeff Henley and Ray Lane. Ray Lane, a former manager at the consulting firm of Booz Allen Hamilton, brought discipline and process, concepts previously foreign to Oracle. Ray took Oracle, a single-product technology company, and worked with Larry to retarget it, to build a complete product line and to concentrate on building brand for the company. Then, Ray Lane hired a team of professional managers under him to speed Oracle's transition to maturity. At the same time, Jeff Henley brought discipline to the operations side of the business. His expertise was critical as Oracle restated earnings, mollified Wall Street, and set new, more stringent accounting policies.

At a time when many were pointing fingers, Larry's decision to bring in professionals required brains, guts, and humility. When he realized that he couldn't solve the company's problems himself, instead of working with insiders or consultants who would just say yes and execute his plans, Larry chose outsiders who could and would do what was necessary to get Oracle back on track. Gaining an outside perspective can benefit any organization that finds itself in a period of difficulty.

Get operations involved

Although the company had always promoted first class when it came to activities and attitudes, Oracle had gotten excessive. Much of the staff was flying first class, even on short trips, and staying in the most expensive hotels. Instead of watching money, everyone seemed to be wasting it—in every area of the company. Given the company's weak financial position, Oracle operations made some tough decisions. It created new travel policies and hardware procurement policies, and actually enforced them—even with the sales team!

Employees quickly adjusted to the new internal policies because everyone realized that now it was important to exercise spending control. However, externally, Oracle did not appear to really falter. Its regional seminars were still hosted in the best hotels in town, although the number of seminars held was reduced and the company still took high-potential customers to dinner, although not as frequently.

Today, Oracle's financials are strong, but the company still maintains some of the internal policies put in place during its time of crisis. For example, only a handful of executives fly first class and all hardware purchases must have managerial approval. Externally, however, Oracle continues to operate in first-class style, as is evident by its annual developer/user conference that costs the company hundreds of thousands of dollars each year.

What Oracle operations did is a good lesson in doing the right thing at the right time. Without changing the external corporate persona, the company was able to appeal to internal individuals to exercise spending restraint.

Focus on customer care

With Oracle stock at an all-time low, Larry Ellison began promoting product quality and customer care. This new attention was well received externally, if not internally where employees complained about being implicitly accused of not caring about customers. At this critical time, the focus on customer care was absolutely necessary. The issue at the forefront, Oracle created a formal product testing process that has had a positive maturing effect on the company, leading to more thorough product testing and recognition of the highest level of product quality and processes in the form of ISO certification.

In reality, Oracle's posture toward customer care did not change very much at the time, but by promoting it, Larry managed to draw the attention away from Oracle's financial difficulties onto something more positive. As he did in competitive situations, Larry reset the battle, giving corporate customers a continued reason to select Oracle as their provider of database technology. As public relations has matured, most companies now understand the value of deflecting negative attention, as Larry did, and replacing it with an activity or process that the company does well.

Lay people off

Days after the crash, Larry and the executives took a hard look at the whole organization and laid off about 10 percent of Oracle's work force. Surprisingly, this had a positive impact on the company that had gotten excessive. It not only got rid of employees who were not performing, but it shed light on the people in the organization who were working harder to support the nonperformers. The new Oracle—the one that emerged from the crash—was leaner and stronger. Several of the people whom I spoke with who were at Oracle during the crash and are there now would like to see the company repeat the layoff process because they believe that laying people off on a more regular basis would keep the company healthy.

Although layoffs can create tension and cause a slight panic in the organization, most actually benefit the organization that remains. The reason is because those who aren't performing are terminated and those who panic and don't believe in the restructuring generally find another job more suitable for them. Employee layoffs mean making tough decisions that generally benefit the organization in the long term.

Learn the Hard Lessons

The Oracle crash was inevitable; it was just a matter of time. The stock price crash was a bracing splash of cold water for Oracle. Many believe that if the stock crash had not happened, Oracle would not be as well positioned as it is today. The crash was a wake-up call, reminding Larry and Oracle that they are fallible.

Oracle learned the hard way that it had to:

- Bring in mature management to handle serious problems
- Enforce rigor in the organization
- Address serious problems promptly
- Focus employees on the positives of making customers happy
- Make hard decisions and stick to them

Fix Weaknesses and Forge Ahead

Were these strategies that Oracle's employed successful? The proof is in the numbers. Today, Oracle is a profitable, $8 billion organization that owns the database market and represents one of just a couple of companies who could stand up to Microsoft.

One thing to note is that Oracle was lucky the crash happened when it did, at a time when the economy was in a recession. Because of the recession, fewer large corporate customers were investing in information technology infrastructure like database technology. As a result, Oracle didn't lose a huge market opportunity as it was rebuilding itself, and Oracle's competitors could not capitalize as much on Oracle's misfortune because they were working hard to keep their own earnings up. In contrast to Informix stock's recent fall when the market and competitors are strong, Oracle was not exposed to the predatory tactics of others.

While every company is unique, the one lesson all companies can learn from Oracle is this: Every successful company must, at some point, make a transition to a principled business machine. A time comes in every fast-growing company when it can no longer operate as an entrepreneurial operation. For some companies, that time means a current CEO must step aside, for others it means that operations must set and enforce policies, and for still others, it means that some of the people who helped the company get to its current position are no longer the best employees for the job and need to be terminated. Whatever the indication is, it is important to recognize the value of a professional management team and to engage them to take a proven vision and turn it into a serious ongoing business concern.

CHAPTER ELEVEN

Exploring
New Markets

B Y THE END OF 1991, ORACLE HAD WEATH-ERED THE CRASH, AND IT WAS TIME TO GO ON THE OFFENSIVE AGAIN. The traditional competitors didn't represent that much threat any more. And besides, Oracle was ready to grow beyond being just a "one-product" company. Oracle was ready to see what new areas could be approached with the company's deep database expertise. Thinking big, Ellison set his sites on getting his company in front of every consumer in the world.

He had a long way to go. At that time, Oracle commissioned a *Wall Street Journal* study regarding the public awareness of Oracle as a company. The results found that awareness of Oracle among *Wall Street Journal* readers was very low. Less than 1 percent of *Journal* readers had heard of Oracle, the fourth largest software company in the world at the time, and of those, only a few knew what the company actually did. In light of this information, Oracle instigated a public relations effort to build a brand name for the company. The only problem was that Oracle didn't have a rich war chest to devote to the effort, and building a brand is expensive.

Dreaming of Interactive Television

The opportunity for Oracle to present itself to the average consumer came in 1993, when Larry created Oracle's New Media division. The charter for the division was to develop database applications for all sorts of different data. While traditional Oracle databases stored rows and columns of numbers and letters, the New Media division was created to build database software to store audio, video, and graphics, as well as huge catalogs of text.

From a product perspective, the goal was to expand Oracle's breadth from simply managing numbers and letters to managing any kind of information in any format. One of the significant technical breakthroughs that Oracle's New Media team accomplished early on was to build a database that could "stream" data out in real time. This meant that now an Oracle database could store digital video (a movie, for example) and deliver it to a large number of different users, simultaneously.

Oracle's new use for its database technology immediately caught the attention of telephone companies wanting to offer video on-demand to their customers and telephone carriers wanting to find a new business that would use up bandwidth on their network to expand product offerings beyond simple voice for telephone calls. Even before the media server technology was completely designed and ready for use, leaders in these markets, including Bell Atlantic, USWest, and British Telecom, had invested in the Oracle New Media development project.

Externally, Larry used every opportunity to tout the benefits of Oracle's new technology that could make any video, any time, available to any consumer. He talked about enabling home shopping with a personal shopper, as well as home banking and all kinds of consumer interactivity. With Oracle's technology, consumers would no longer need a personal computer; they could use the television as their interface. All of a sudden, Oracle was poised to make the leap from the air-conditioned back office of the corporate Fortune 2000 into the homes and minds of consumers all over the world—to the "Consumer Six Billion." Ellison had created the Excitement Factor again.

Internally, Larry embraced the project just as enthusiastically, code naming it "Alexandria" after the world's first library in Alexandria, Egypt. Oracle team members even had T-shirts embossed with the division's ambitious slogan, "Changing the World."

Like a wild fire, Oracle's new direction caught the attention of the industry and the press alike. Fueled by Larry's exciting new vision and partnerships with industry leaders Bell Atlantic, USWest, British Telecom, Sega, Apple Computer, cable set-top providers, and even media companies like Disney, the coverage poured out. The ground swell even caught Oracle by surprise; a marketing person for the Media Server group recalled, "We were getting calls from Todd Rundgren (popular music star and Hollywood media personality) and we weren't returning his calls because we were so busy—any normal person wouldn't do that!"

When Larry saw that he had struck a chord that resonated with the press, he continued to play it. The company quickly organized a glitzy Los Angeles multimedia announcement for the technology, and Larry personally anchored the event. Walter Cronkite accompanied as a featured guest. The event, held in the Capital Cities/ABC complex, promised live demonstrations of Larry's brave new vision. Limousines arrived. On stage, Larry watched movie clips, ordered pizza, and bought a new sweater for his mother, all from the user interface of his television. And most importantly, all with exciting video stored on an Oracle database. Instantly, the New Media revolution propelled Oracle into the limelight.

Despite all of the excitement, Oracle's New Media group was not going to be able to ship a real product for the foreseeable future. Nevertheless, the image that the New Media technology represented extended Oracle and its products beyond the walls of the information management classification where the company had always been.

The vice president of marketing for the New Media group explained, "New Media's value was not in the technology that it created, but rather in the kind of customers who were exposed to Oracle. The creation of Java and the dream of having a universal language for every computer did the same for Sun. New Media allowed Oracle and Larry to talk at a higher level with these new customers. Where Oracle had been communicating with senior people in the Information Services department, it now had another reason to break through to the CEO."

For example, at the time, British Telecom (BT) was Oracle's largest customer in the United Kingdom. Until BT signed onto Oracle's New Media project, Oracle sales teams and executives had not been able to get a meeting with BT's chief technical officer. Once BT and Oracle agreed to collaborate, he was a regular on the Oracle campus and even hosted a team of Oracle engineers into his private residence in the United Kingdom so that they could install the first demonstration unit outside of an Oracle building—in his living room.

Another benefit Oracle had not foreseen when it established the New Media division was the reaction of its competitors. While Informix and Sybase were continuing to challenge Oracle's technical leadership in the traditional database product field, the New Media announcement caught them completely off guard. Even Microsoft didn't know how to respond to Oracle's bold new vision! And in fact, none of the companies were able to respond for almost a year, and when competitive announcements finally came they were watered down versions of what Oracle had presented and were not as well received by customers or the press.

There are five distinct traits that made the New Media effort so successful:

- It was first to market
- It had a dramatic, clearly articulated vision and visual demonstration
- Larry Ellison personally got involved
- It created a new technology playing field to which competitors were slow to respond
- The effort was validated by well-recognized partners

Although Oracle invested heavily in the marketing of New Media, the company never bet the business on the effort. Instead, Oracle held onto the core database market and kept the New Media effort separate and distinct. In fact, the market for digital video products is still emerging, and Oracle was able to see that, too. The benefit of the New Media strategy for Oracle was great marketing exposure without the risk of losing its core, profitable business.

One thing is clear. Whether or not the division would have ever released a product is irrelevant. The New Media division was a huge success for Oracle. As the vice president of marketing for New Media division said, "The New Media Division cost one-fifth of what it would have taken Oracle to go out and buy the same amount of brand awareness through advertising."

With the New Media effort, Oracle was able to take the lead and break down barriers, to see a future in its existing database products. Regardless of whether you ever ship a revolutionary product, presenting a compelling future vision positions you as a leader.

Taking on Microsoft with the Network Computer

By 1995, Oracle's New Media group had grown to more than 300 employees. When it became clear that the world's communications and content development infrastructure was not prepared to spend hundreds of millions of dollars for the Oracle software required to power interactive television, changes had to be made within Oracle to reduce the tremendous cost of the interactive television project. However, the employees Oracle had transferred or hired into the New Media group were all handpicked by Larry Ellison, so a simple reduction in force was out of the question. Larry met with the head of the New Media team and told him to go off and think of some new direction to take his oversized group. Despite its lack of success in interactive television, Larry was still willing to take another chance at creating new markets for Oracle or at least to move Oracle into new areas.

Eliminating the Competition from Your Deals

The next time they met, the head of New Media presented a number of new ideas to Larry. The one that immediately caught Larry's attention was a database appliance. The vision was that Oracle software generated a great deal of related hardware, software, and services sales that didn't benefit Oracle. It was not uncommon to hear of a deal where Oracle had sold $5 million in software as the heart of a new inventory database, but that the related sales around the deployment of that database were as follows:

$4 million = New server machine to run Oracle Server database

$4 million = New PC workstations to enable user access

$1 million = New PC software (MS-Windows, MS-Office, etc.)

$1 million = New networking hardware to establish connections from PCs to server

$8 million = Related programming, data conversion, training, and support

In this conservative example, while Oracle generated revenues of $5 million for itself, it generated revenues of $18 million for other companies. Often, it was the sale of the Oracle database and application that justified the purchase of the Oracle software and the purchase of all of the related items. However, the most annoying element of this and other examples for Oracle was that the company had enabled a large sale for looming competitor Microsoft.

Clearly, enabling Microsoft purchases and helping to establish Microsoft as the PC platform in large corporations was contrary to Oracle's best interests. Further, many of these PCs were used for just one purpose: to allow the user to gain access to an Oracle database. It was not at all uncommon to visit a customer site and see countless PCs with the database application literally burned into the screen because that was the sole function that the PC performed.

At this point, Microsoft was not looking for allies. It had made its intentions clear: releasing Microsoft Windows NT, which was openly aimed at becoming the operating system platform on which enterprises could run their big servers. Additionally, Microsoft had licensed core technology from database vendor Sybase upon which Microsoft was building SQL Server, a direct competitor to Oracle.

The solution that the head of the New Media group proposed showed Oracle cutting Microsoft out of the picture. Instead of using PCs, customers would buy Oracle-developed workstation hardware and software that was optimized just to run Oracle database applications. The concept would mean some earth-shattering discontinuities in the way that applications were managed inside businesses, but it would make millions more for Oracle. Specifically, the head of New Media proposed a database appliance that would be:

1. Easy to use. Oracle's specialized computers would have function keys that would make database functions like "Search" and "Report" single-step processes for an end user.

2. Less expensive than a PC. The computers Oracle would develop would be less expensive than current

PCs because they would be designed to run only one application. Oracle's head of New Media estimated that by eliminating much of the hard disk storage, RAM capacity, and internals from the PC, it could lower the price to under $1,000, which was three times less than a moderately equipped PC at the time. And if Oracle was clever, the company could devise a system where applications could be loaded from across the network, eliminating the cost of the diskette or CD-ROM drive and reducing the cost of the workstation even further.

3. Easy to administer. At the time, individual analyst studies put the total cost of ownership per machine at more than $10,000 per year, with only $3,000 of that cost coming from hardware acquisition. The bulk of the remaining cost came from system support, upgrade, and maintenance. A database appliance solution could help manage the high cost of PC ownership. If Oracle could make the applications load from across the network instead of having to install them manually by diskette or CD-ROM, the company could enable system administrators to deliver application updates to these workstations very easily. And by building the hardware to support just database applications, Oracle would not have to worry about all of the complexity that MS-Windows machines faced with application conflicts, hardware conflicts, and configuration issues.

In sum, the proposal for Oracle to build a database workstation appliance showed that it would make working with Oracle databases better, cheaper, faster, easier to use, and more manageable than a Windows PC. Best of all, Oracle could "own" the entire enterprise computing infrastructure—end to end—and Microsoft Windows, which had a tight stranglehold on the workstation, would instantly become unnecessary. People would buy Oracle's devices for the applications they performed, and the operating system would be completely invisible to the end user.

The vision was sweeping and Oracle's New Media team was well positioned for the job. Although most of Oracle's employees had no direct experience with building hardware, the New Media team had worked closely with manufacturers such as Apple, Philips, and Lucky-Goldstar for the past two years developing set-top box hardware for interactive television. Adapting that experience to building a hardware platform for the Oracle database appliance was going to be relatively easy, as many of the problems had already been solved. And while Oracle did not have expertise in developing operating system software, there were a number of viable options available for licensing, at little cost. Once those two issued were solved, Oracle would have an offering it could position as a strong alternative to the Microsoft/Intel PC. The New Media team, with the technology and expertise in place, estimated that it could have a working prototype within months and the first production product in a little over a year. The proposal was a success, but the implementation was headed for disaster.

Lessons Learned from the Network Computer

Though Oracle did not sell millions of network computers, the company did accumulate a number of good lessons from the experience that will surely be applied to future ventures.

Keeping boundaries around a good idea

The database appliance concept made Larry Ellison ecstatic. In one deft move, he could retarget the unsuccessful interactive television effort at a new target, one that would be even more complementary to Oracle's core business of selling database software to large enterprises, while offering those accounts an alternative to buying software from Microsoft. But as the days passed, Larry thought more about the idea and it wasn't enough. Larry wanted to take Microsoft head-on. He wanted to add more and more to the simple concept of a database appliance. Soon, the call came down from his office to add a word processing package to the new idea. Then a spreadsheet. Communications, e-mail, and a Web browser were next. Within days, the very simple concept of a one-application device had evolved into a complete replacement for a Windows PC with all of the same or more functionality.

Suddenly, the development task of creating a simple database appliance had increased exponentially. Database applications were something that Oracle developers felt that they had the expertise to create in short order. Spreadsheets and word processors were programs that took years to build, test, gather usage models on, and perfect. The Oracle developers working on the project would need time to understand the subtleties of creating that kind of software as it was well outside of their normal scope. Further, the hardware requirements for a whole new set of applications were going to be much greater than what was necessary to run a single database application. Most importantly, the complexity of the entire project increased dramatically. Planning had to be devoted to how the applications would work together, how they would share information, how users would move from function to function, and more. A small number of simple sounding requests made the project dramatically more complex—and more work!

When you decide to make a move into a new market, remember Oracle's network computer lesson. The successful strategy calls for articulating a broad vision but delivering on it incrementally—not all at once!

Announcing early wakes the incumbent

Just as the team was beginning to plan how it would deliver this grand new product, Larry Ellison dubbed the new idea the "Network Computer" and pre-announced it to the press. He told the world it would be available in a year and that it would cost less than $1,000. This was not just a teaser or a preview, Larry laid out the whole strategy. His vision of the network computer was that it would change the world. And it would bring computing to every person because it would be available at such a low cost and would be so easy to manage even as the numbers of users scaled beyond the millions. What Larry also articulated was how it would replace the PC and make Microsoft Windows unnecessary.

In the early days of Oracle, Larry always announced products well ahead of their time. We are reminded again that, "Larry's world is 18 months ahead of others." Just as Oracle was releasing one version of the database, Larry was announcing what features and functionality would be included in the next. Then, however, he had the benefit of being in the lead. Customers who were just figuring out how they would take advantage of all of the good new features that Oracle had released in its current database version were comforted to know that Oracle had a vision for what was next, and that by the time they wanted something,

Oracle would probably have it. That practice was one of the early ways Oracle established its perception of leadership in the database industry. In many ways, it forced Oracle's competitors to compete with Oracle's vision and not with Oracle's shipping products.

The media's reaction to Oracle's network computer announcement was mixed. The cadre of press opposed to Microsoft flocked to the announcement with the hope of a new regime that promised to make the world free from Redmond. Others were skeptical. A heated debate ensued, and whether people loved or hated the idea (few were on the fence), the brash announcement drew a great deal of attention to Oracle.

Although attention from the press is generally good, in this case it exposed many of the elements of Oracle's strategy that had not yet been thought through within the organization. Who was going to manufacture these brave new devices? How was Oracle going to sell them? How was Oracle going to support them? On a more personal level, people wanted to know how to compare their PC spreadsheet with the one that Oracle was going to deliver on the network computer.

Oracle didn't panic, but it didn't have all of the answers to these difficult questions either. It quickly became obvious to those close to the project that Oracle had promised more than it could deliver. And as time passed, most people came to believe that the idea of the network computer was more a dream than reality.

It is possible that Oracle could have succeeded with its network computer project if the company hadn't pre-announced it. By presenting it too early, however, Oracle never gave the project a chance. In the market for workstations, Oracle was not the leader. Microsoft and Intel were the leaders. They had been hard at work for more than fifteen years perfecting the personal computer and knew many of the potential pitfalls. They knew the hard questions to present to Oracle and the media, questions that Oracle would only be able to answer if the company had strong expertise in the area. But Oracle's team was not ready for the interrogation. Faced with an early announcement about a product that it had not had time to think through and an established competitor, Oracle fell short.

Don't fall short. If you are facing an entrenched competitor, keep your offering secret until you are ready to come out with something clearly superior.

Presenting the competition with a problem encourages them to solve it

What Oracle may not have considered enough when it pre-announced the network computer was Microsoft's reaction. Microsoft did not take the challenge lightly. It had finally pushed Apple into a niche spot in the personal computer market, and it was not willing to open the door to another competitor.

Externally, Microsoft did everything it could do to make Oracle's network computer announcement appear vacant and impossible. Internally, Microsoft examined Oracle's positioning closely. Oracle had found weak spots in the personal computer. PCs were expensive, hard to use, and costly to administer and support. Even if Oracle failed with its network computer initiative, another competitor, potentially Apple or Hewlett-Packard, might come up with a product that did answer the Microsoft deficiencies that Oracle highlighted.

As a result, Microsoft mounted three efforts:

1. *Reduce PC cost.* Microsoft met with chip maker Intel and other computer providers, including Dell, Compaq, and Gateway, to strategize on how to counter the Oracle network computer effort. The announcement had not gone unnoticed with hardware providers. Their reaction was clear and swift. The chip manufacturers moved to integrate components as tightly as they could. Where there were previously three chips, there would be one that did the work of the three, for the cost of just one. This strategy reduced the cost of the components necessary to build PCs and the time and cost it took to create and test one. It also reduced the number of elements that could fail inside of a PC, increasing its reliability. The chip maker and hardware manufacturers also went to their suppliers and redoubled their demand for lower cost hard drives, monitors, and memory. The network computer threat was a tremendously cohesive force for the computer manufacturers.

2. *Improve PC usability.* Microsoft's core applications— Excel, Word, and PowerPoint—had continued to add feature after feature as a result of the competition Microsoft faced from Lotus, Word Perfect, and other off-the-shelf productivity application providers. What these applications had failed to do, however, was to organize new features in a way that still made basic functionality accessible to a novice user. Faced with the challenge of a new, simpler device, Microsoft set out to improve the user experience for all of its core

applications. It would make the user interface easier to understand and use for beginners and make more complex features visible only to more sophisticated users who knew how to access them.

The hardware manufacturers rallied to solve the ease of use problem as well. They did extensive user testing to see what issues kept new PC buyers from getting their machines up and running quickly. As a result of this research, they did a number of critical things to make the "out-of-the-box" experience as painless as possible, including creating simple graphical color documentation and friendly icons on cables and plugs so setting up a new machine could be done by a novice. They also offered pre-installed software on some machines so that a machine could be used the minute that it was taken out of the box and turned on. And they increased the quality of their support employees so that they could handle requests from users who had never had experience with a computer.

3. *Improve PC administration.* Even before the network computer announcement, Microsoft had known that Windows-based PCs were hard to configure, support, and manage. Aside from the research studies that showed high cost of ownership, its own users were clamoring for software that was not so difficult to set up. Largely in response to the network computer, however, Microsoft launched its "Zero Admin" initiative. It was exactly what Microsoft users were hoping for. The goal of the initiative was to extend Microsoft Windows such that an installation would not require any further administration. And Microsoft began a

series of projects, some on its own and some in conjunction with hardware manufacturers, to create new installation technology called the Install Shield to standardize the way that software is added to a PC. Microsoft also created software that would automatically sense when new hardware was installed into the machine and would configure it automatically as well. Finally, Microsoft began to work on remote administration tools so that a support person in a different location could log onto a remote computer and make changes to it if something went wrong.

Although Oracle did begin working on a product that attempted to meet Larry's vision of the network computer by establishing relationships with hardware manufactures and writing software, the challenges Oracle faced continued to mount. The scope of the project continued to broaden, and soon the vision for the network computing platform included set-top boxes that brought the Internet to a television and screen phones optimized for consumer access to the Internet.

Organizationally, the company also faced challenges as Larry created not just an independent division, as he had in the past with successful products, but an independent company focused on the network computer. But employees who went to work at NCI (Network Computer, Inc.) received stock in Oracle, rather than the independent entity. Incubating the network computing effort partly inside of the company and partly outside proved to be an ineffective solution because employees had none of the autonomy of being an independent entity. These employees were also motivated through the stock plan to make Oracle, rather than NCI, successful. It was a solution that benefited very few.

The next time that you articulate a shortcoming of a competitor's product, you need to know that your competitive advantage has a shelf life. Either your claim is without merit, in which case the competitor will debunk it as quickly as they can, or your claim will cause your competitor to enhance their offering. Either way, you need to make the most of your advantage while you have it.

Give sales something they can sell

Even without a product to sell, Oracle's sales efforts for the network computer began immediately after the announcement. The theory was that the huge and highly trained Oracle sales force would provide great demand for the product, thereby justifying more resources be spent on it and pressing the development team to release a product. The problem was that the Oracle's sales force was constructed to sell expensive software. In stark contrast, the network computer was an inexpensive piece of hardware with software included.

While the compensation plans and training and support infrastructure were perfect for database software; they were all wrong for selling a commodity hardware product. As if that were not enough, Oracle quickly decided that it was not going to offer the hardware directly, that it was going to encourage its hardware manufacturing licensees to build hardware that Oracle would sell. All that the Oracle sales representatives could sell was the software for the NC, at roughly a $10 per unit price. For a salesperson used to selling database software at a cost of hundreds of thousands of dollars per license, this was a complete mismatch. Despite pleas from Oracle management, the salespeople refused to promote the

Oracle NC and Oracle was forced to create a special team of sales representatives who worked exclusively on selling the NC.

Before Oracle ever released a production NC, Microsoft, Intel and the PC manufacturers came up with solutions to the issues the product addressed—price, manageability, and ease of use. And at an internal Oracle meeting in June of 1998, Larry Ellison formally announced that the NC was dead.

With more planning and preparation, it is easy to see how this story could have played the other direction for Oracle. Had Oracle silently gone to work on the NC, waiting to awaken the sleeping PC industry giants, the company would have been able to come to market with a coherent vision, strategy, and product. Oracle may have changed the way people view and use Microsoft Windows and PCs today.

But in combination, many of the factors that had worked previously for Oracle—pre-announcing a product, setting up a separate development organization, and aggressive selling—now worked against it. The reason Oracle failed now is because it was operating in a more mature marketplace. The market leader, Microsoft, and PC vendors had already established the rules, yet Oracle sought to unseat these leader with its NC announcement.

This episode proved an important lesson to Oracle. If Oracle is going to continue to grow at its current pace, the company must continue to look for new businesses, inevitably confronting the biggest player in the software business: Microsoft. Look around in your own market. If you are going to own it, you must ultimately take on and defeat all those in it as well as those who may enter.

CHAPTER TWELVE

The All or Nothing Future

May you live in exciting times.
—ANCIENT CHINESE PROVERB

F OR ORACLE, ALL OF THE CHALLENGES, ALL OF THE VICTORIES, AND ALL OF THE HARD-FOUGHT BATTLES HAVE MERELY BEEN PREPARATION. Like a boxer taking on stronger and stronger opponents, learning new moves and becoming more facile, Oracle is now prepared to enter the championship ring. This time the opponent is Microsoft—and the prize is survival.

The Inevitable Clash

A brief look at technology history reveals that the Oracle-Microsoft clash was inevitable. This chapter is not about lessons from Oracle's past but more of a look into Oracle's future. Oracle started building software for an IBM mainframe, the largest machine on the market, while Microsoft started building software for the smallest machine, the IBM PC. As time passed, Oracle adapted its software to a wide range of smaller and smaller computers, including machines running Microsoft's operating system software. To counter Oracle, Microsoft pushed its Windows NT operating system software onto larger and larger machines.

Concurrently, Microsoft began an even more directed effort to thwart Oracle. In the late 1980s, Microsoft licensed database software technology from Oracle's competitor,

Sybase, and began building a direct competitor to the Oracle database. The Microsoft branded product carried the same name as its Sybase cousin, SQL Server. When it appeared on the market, SQL Server was not much of a technical threat to Oracle because it only ran on Microsoft operating systems, which made it inherently limited in the amount of data it could hold and the number of users it could support. But anxious to begin the assault on Oracle, Microsoft knew exactly what to do when Oracle branded it a technically inferior product. Microsoft sold it cheap. Unlike Oracle's traditional database competitors—Informix and Ingres—Microsoft didn't have to worry about making money on its SQL Server product. Rather, Microsoft could focus on making money in the operating system market, where it had no strong competitors and could use SQL Server to apply pressure to all of the database vendors. Microsoft's strategy was well targeted because it allowed the company to do three things:

Drive down prices

Oracle, Sybase, and the other database vendors had high fixed-cost structures to support. Aside from having sophisticated technical teams to create the core technology, all of the database companies also had to invest in large porting organizations, which adapted the databases to different computing platforms. Although a great expense, the technical teams paled in comparison to the amount of money that the database vendors invested in building direct sales forces. For example, the Oracle sales force today is more than 10,000 people strong, and as discussed in previous chapters, the organization's employees are well compensated. As soon as Microsoft introduced its inexpensive SQL

Server, customers had more leverage to negotiate pricing with Oracle and the other vendors. Few customers would have chosen the first version of SQL Server for an industrial-strength enterprise application, but the threat was enough to begin eroding Oracle's price structure.

Gain installed base

Although enterprise customers with large financial or inventory applications did not adopt Microsoft SQL Server, prospects on a tighter budget did. These organizations fell into two categories: small companies and developers. Before Microsoft offered SQL Server, neither developers nor small companies had a choice. They had to pay Oracle's high prices, Oracle's competitor's high prices, or do without. Microsoft gave them both a choice and reassurance, as Microsoft promised the market that over time the Windows NT operating system with SQL Server would scale to larger machines and be able to accommodate more users and more data. Microsoft also understood that both categories of companies would be valuable to it over time. Small companies would grow, while developers would build applications that would be sold to larger companies. Microsoft was willing to provide all of these other organizations with its database software at a low price to gain their early loyalty.

Begin deep product integration

Aside from pushing prices down and accumulating users, the most deadly threat Microsoft presents to Oracle today is that of database integration (and bundling) with Microsoft's operating system. The combined offering of Microsoft's Windows NT and SQL Server database presents a double danger to Oracle. Today, a customer has to make a conscious choice whether to buy SQL Server because it is sold separately. Part of making that choice means that customers are likely to at least consider other alternatives, such as Oracle. If and when the database comes integrated with the operating system, Microsoft SQL Server will be the default choice. Witness what happened to NetScape when Internet Explorer was bundled into Windows. Given that SQL Server costs less, there would have to be something seriously technically wrong with it for a customer to consider Oracle. This does not bode well for Oracle.

Another danger Oracle faces is that once Microsoft integrates its own database product into Windows NT, it will be harder for Oracle to make its database run well on Windows NT. This is a subtle but critical point. Oracle relies on the creator of the operating system software to make the underlying technology available for the database to use. For example, part of what an Oracle database does is write database information to a computer's hard disk. When the database does that, it uses a command from the operating system to perform the action. Today, Microsoft makes those commands available to companies like Oracle in the form of developer software and documentation. What the operating system does with that command once Oracle has issued it is out of Oracle's control. In light of the findings that have come out of the Department of Justice's investigation of Microsoft, where specific instances of Microsoft withholding operating system information from would-be competitors have arisen, this is a big risk factor for Oracle.

In a worst case scenario, it is possible to imagine that Windows NT developers could build two such commands that both do the same thing, with one exception. One of the commands would only be available to developers inside of Microsoft, while the other was available to the general public, including Oracle. Further, imagine that the command that was offered only to developers inside Microsoft would be more efficient than the one made available to the general public. In that scenario, it would be impossible for Oracle to build a database that was as fast as Microsoft's SQL Server when both ran on the same Windows NT machine.

Just as Oracle was able to outflank many of its earlier competitors by committing itself to making its software available on every possible platform, Microsoft may be able to outflank Oracle through the company's domination in operating systems.

In today's rapidly changing business environment, these kind of challenges—competitive risks and opportunities—exist in almost every market category. Look, for example, at the battle being fought over access to long-distance and local phone services. Or, the cable and utility industries attempts to outflank the phone companies in competing for customer's Internet access business.

Every enterprise must keep its head up and eyes open for this kind of "flanking maneuver" on the part of its competition—both present and future—or be left in the dust with no revenue, customers, or market share.

Understanding Microsoft's Strengths

Aside from "owning" and controlling the operating system platform, Microsoft has some unique strengths that Oracle will have to face.

Capital

At the writing of this book, Microsoft has a war chest of $15 billion in the bank. Oracle has less than one-tenth of that amount. With that capital, Microsoft can afford to watch the technology market unfold, and if something looks promising, buy it. Microsoft no longer has to make speculative technology bets, it just has to be able to recognize a trend, like the Internet, once it has been established and then acquire it.

Development team

Probably more valuable than its bank account is the team of developers that Microsoft has accumulated in Redmond, Washington, and around the world. Because Microsoft products include operating system, word processing, Internet, commerce, and even video production software, Microsoft has great technical depth from which to pull when it wants to create new products in any market area. Having focused its business primarily on database software, Oracle does not have the same wide range of technical expertise.

Retail distribution channel

Most Microsoft products are not sold by Microsoft. They are sold by hardware manufacturers, including Compaq and Dell, which include Microsoft software with every computer they ship. Microsoft products are also sold by retail outlets, such as EggHead and Fry's, to consumers or businesses wanting to upgrade versions of Microsoft Word or to purchase Microsoft Project. Using third parties to distribute its products, Microsoft has been able to achieve broad distribution without incurring the overhead associated with retail stores and direct salespeople. Oracle field sales handles the majority of Oracle's sales, which are mostly to fortune 500 accounts.

Consumer understanding

No software company employs the art of consumer marketing, branding, and awareness in the way that companies like Proctor & Gamble have. But within the category of software, Microsoft has devoted untold effort and money to understanding what consumers respond to in marketing, advertising, and new products. With that knowledge, some name recognition, and a market lead, Microsoft has an advantage over companies like Oracle when consumers buy computers and software.

Although the previous items may make it appear that Microsoft has already won, Oracle has its own advantages. And it's not over yet.

Evaluating Oracle's Strengths

If there is one software company—and powerful leader—that may be strong enough to unseat Microsoft, it's Oracle. The reason is because Oracle has a number of strengths that are unique to it.

Direct sales force

Oracle has built direct relationships with customers. The Armani-clad Oracle field sales representatives personally know the customers who buy their software. They understand the business problems that their customer face and they have established a rapport with customers. These personal relationships give Oracle an advantage in situations where it faces Microsoft in head-to-head competition.

Consulting force

Oracle's consulting force is a tremendous asset to the company. Although the organization took years to build, it has been extremely successful in enabling Oracle sales representatives to deliver to customers exactly the solution they want and to charge extra for it. Aside from being profitable, Oracle's consultants offer an on-site Oracle presence at customer locations. Simply being there is a big advantage for Oracle in the battle of understanding customer requirements and learning about new opportunities within an existing account.

Enterprise application understanding

The business of providing enterprise applications is difficult. These applications are built for power and getting the job done as quickly, efficiently, and as reliably as possible. There is an art to building applications that are suitable for industrial, enterprise use. And Oracle understands it. Users in corporate environments expect an application to step them through the task at hand, to check their entries, to be managed by a central administrator and to be up and running for as long as they are at work. These requirements may seem obvious, but Oracle has spent the last twenty years building both expertise and credibility in this area.

Installed base

For business use today, Oracle's database is the standard. It is not used by every company in every situation, but it is the measure against which other vendors are compared. Oracle is installed at tens of thousands of locations around the world and at every Fortune 50 account. In many of those businesses, Oracle "owns" the data. There is risk, expense, and effort associated with moving that data into another vendor's software. And for the majority of those businesses, the data that Oracle manages is mission-critical to their organization. This asset is one that Oracle has also worked years to create and it affords the company fertile ground for new short- and long-term product offerings.

Freedom from the PC

Microsoft's legacy is the PC. Five years ago, it was a legacy that any company wanted. And today, analysts are predicting that the apex of the PC is either here or near. Demand has been nearly filled for these one-size-fits-all devices and it seems likely that the world will begin to turn to devices that are more specialized to certain tasks than a PC. If indeed the PC was to be replaced in the near future, Oracle would be well poised to provide an alternative offering to the market. Oracle has never tied itself to any computing platform. In fact, quite the opposite, Oracle has relied on computer platform technology to continue to change, and in the case of the network computer, the company has even tried to accelerate that change on its own. Oracle's history of adapting to a changing market position it well to be free from the PC.

Expertise

Oracle's development team is focused. It has a tremendous amount of expertise in building software that is well suited for industrial use. Software that is reliable, scalable to large numbers of users, and well integrated with the other industrial-strength hardware and software that corporations use to run their businesses. Over time, Oracle has developed practices that guarantee every product that the company delivers can meet the needs of enterprise users. A focus on quality control bodes well for keeping customers satisfied with a particular vendor's products.

Friends (or common enemies)

In the spirit of rallying against a common foe, Oracle has accumulated some very big friends. IBM, Sun Microsystems, and Netscape are among the companies that have already worked with Oracle in an attempt to stop Microsoft from expanding into enterprise computing. Drawn together by a common enemy, the combined power of these companies and smaller organizations that work with them offers substantially more resources than Microsoft could have any time in the foreseeable future.

Finding Strategies that Amplify Oracle's Advantages

Like many large companies that are faced with a strong competitor, Oracle must continue to execute while at the same time innovate. But what will Oracle do to protect its established base within corporate America? What can it offer to the consumer six billion in the way of exciting new products? How will Oracle maintain its relevance? Predicting exactly what Oracle will do is unrealistic, especially given that Larry Ellison enjoys unexpected, unconventional attacks. However, I believe that there are some areas where Oracle may be able to set a new agenda and challenge Microsoft.

Looking at Hosted Applications

One of the trends Oracle has initiated with its Oracle 8i, a new Internet database product, is hosted applications.

Instead of selling packaged application software, such as an inventory application, to a company and having that company purchase the necessary server and networking hardware, Oracle may choose to offer that company an opportunity to run its applications at Oracle. With hosted applications, Oracle would run the customers' application in its own computer center. Oracle would buy the machines and the networking hardware and hire employees to manage, maintain, support and backup this application. Employees within the customer company would use a Web browser on their workstation to connect to the application server at Oracle. The Web browser would actually run the application. Then, employees at the customer site would enter and interact with the data, which is stored at Oracle's computer center. If employees at the customer site have questions about how to use the application, they would call Oracle's technical support center.

From a customer perspective, an Oracle hosted application is attractive because the up-front capital investment is dramatically less. In this scenario, the customer does not have to buy any computing hardware, networking hardware, applications software, or server operating system hardware. Because customers don't have to buy any of these components, they also don't have to worry about how soon the equipment will be obsolete. Nor do they have the expense of replacing broken components or upgrading existing ones, and they don't have to learn the intricacies of installing and administering server hardware and software. Customers also save money on employees because they don't have to build a support staff of application experts. In short, customers can focus on their own business and add additional users to the Oracle hosted application whenever they want, wherever they want.

From the Oracle perspective, there are also many attractive elements to offering hosted applications. At the highest level, Oracle could offer more to a customer than it did before. Hosted applications would enable Oracle to become more closely integrated with the customer's business and establish a higher value proposition with the customer, tying customers even more closely to Oracle then they are now. Oracle could also leverage all of the expertise that it has in development when it creates the applications in the first place. Instead of forcing a customer to learn how to administer and support its applications, Oracle can use the knowledge that it has gained in creating the application to quickly train its own people and extend its service offering. The field sales and support force that Oracle has amassed over the years would also be a huge asset for Oracle both in terms of promoting hosted applications and delivering associated services. And finally, Oracle would get to choose what other software would run on the servers that are hosted at the Oracle computer center. You can bet Oracle won't chose Microsoft Windows NT.

Locking Up Content

The popularity of the Internet has given Oracle an advantage that few other computer vendors can claim. Much of the quality information—referred to as content—on the Internet today is stored in Oracle databases. With the assumption that the Internet will only grow, there is an opportunity for Oracle to even more firmly entrench itself as the de facto storage software standard for major Internet sites. There are only a handful of product enhancements and some pricing changes required. If any company is poised to be this standard, it's Oracle.

Technically, the process for Oracle to be the standard is reasonably straightforward. The most important element would be to integrate the Oracle database more closely with existing Web server software products, including offerings from former network computing partners Netscape and IBM.

The area of pricing would make Oracle's quest a bit more complex. Today, Oracle pricing is organized for large enterprise application use. Take the number of employees in your company who are likely to use the database, multiply that number by Oracle's cost per seat, and that is approximately the license fee. Typically, a cost per seat is around $1,000. In the Internet model, a catalog retailer with a Web site might have 10,000 visitors in a day. There is no way that site can afford to pay Oracle $1,000 for each one of those "users" who connected. Margins on the Web are too slim and other software that the retailer would use to run its site is very inexpensive or even free. Oracle would have to come up with new pricing that is better suited to the Internet model. That pricing would need to be simple to understand, inexpensive, and easy to monitor.

Surveying Integrated Applications

Competition in the field of packaged or off-the-shelf applications is fierce. Vendors specializing in inventory, manufacturing, sales force automation, human resources, and helpdesk applications are far too numerous to count and new companies are popping up every day with a new packaged application offering. All of these products compete with Oracle's own packaged applications products, and many of Oracle's competitors in the applications area use an Oracle database underneath their application. Many businesses around the world have discovered that using a packaged application to run, for example, their inventory system, are now looking at the rest of their enterprise to see what other areas could be improved by using database application software to keep track of it.

Despite its early entry into the market, Oracle's applications group is behind the competition. Dedicated Enterprise Resource Planning (ERP) application providers like SAP and Baan have grown to where they each sell more than five times the amount of applications that Oracle's applications team sells.

Soon customers will be asking for applications for every area of their business. Shipping, receiving, financials, asset management, procurement, and time/project management applications are hot areas for many companies today. Although most of these companies started with an inventory or manufacturing application a couple of years ago, they are becoming more sophisticated in their requests and now want all of their applications to work together. This is where Oracle has an advantage.

The ties between applications are both subtle and complex because there are so many areas in a company where information overlaps. To provide a couple of examples, it is easy to imagine that a consulting manager setting up a time accounting system for her employees would want to be able to access information from the human resources database so that she didn't have to enter and maintain all of the information about each person. It is also easy to imagine that a shipping application would access both the financial and inventory databases so that it could verify and log any products that were shipped out and alert the accounting team to stay on top of tax and import/export data. The examples could go on and on, but the important point is that THE company that can offer a complete set of applications that all work together from a central place will have a tremendous advantage over competitors that only offer one application, for example, a manufacturing application, to customers.

Oracle is in a strong position to both develop and deliver a fully integrated set of complex applications. The company already offers a broad range of packaged applications, including financial, inventory, and manufacturing, so buying or building any missing pieces would not be that difficult. The integration between these components would be challenging, but Oracle's product development team would have as much, if not more, experience than anyone else at delivering projects of this scale. And the company's vast sales force has more experience than anyone else at selling this kind of large-scale project. With 10,000 people in the field, Oracle is looking for powerful solutions to complex problems and products with a big impact that highly paid sales representatives can sell.

Touching on Appliance Devices

It is no secret that Oracle failed on its first foray with the network computer. But the failure was in execution, not the strategic idea around what the company was trying to achieve. Oracle must pursue strategies that result in less expensive, easier ways for customers to access Oracle databases, and ways that make Microsoft software unnecessary. Oracle needs to be thinking about possible PC alternatives for information access. The PC is not going to go away overnight, but there is trend toward information appliance devices, and Oracle has an opportunity to capitalize.

Consider, for example, the PalmPilot connected organizer from 3Com. This pocket-sized calendar and datebook, weighing just six ounces, took Microsoft completely by surprise. The PalmPilot is everything that a Windows PC is not. It is small, light, friendly, easy to use, and offers only a handful of functions (primarily calendaring and address book). But in less than two years, more than two million PalmPilots have been purchased. If industry analyst expectation is correct, the PalmPilot will continue to grow at the same furious rate that it has already established. Furthermore, there isn't a bit of Microsoft software on the PalmPilot. This is an ideal situation for Oracle. Oracle has already started to respond aggressively to building connectivity and database software for the PalmPilot platform, making sure to beat Microsoft to the punch.

But Microsoft also sees the opportunity in non-PC devices. Its acquisition of WebTV shows that as new models for information access emerge, Microsoft will have a presence in those areas as well. Given that Oracle sticks to its core strategy, it has an advantage against Microsoft where non-PC devices are involved. Oracle can focus on being the neutral back-end database for any non-PC device, which by definition makes it the optimal back-end database for all of them. Content creators and service providers, from the *Wall Street Journal* to America Online, want to be able to deliver their content and applications to any user, regardless of whether it is a personal computer or a television. For any of these people, a database that is not limited to a specific set of information appliances will be very appealing.

Forging Partnerships

In the early years, Oracle was brash and very much on its own. It held hardware manufacturers at its mercy and made limited efforts to work with other software manufacturers. Given Microsoft's position in the market today, Oracle now operates differently. During the network computing initiative, Oracle found common ground with IBM, Sun, and Netscape. This kind of collaboration is going to be critical to the future success of Oracle, as well as others.

From the examples I've provided, there are some obvious areas of potential collaboration:

Develop a complete Web server

With the power of these vendors, it should be possible to quickly assemble and integrate all of the components necessary to surpass the functionality—and popularity—of the Microsoft's Site Server software with Windows NT operating system offering. The combination of a Netscape Web server, an Oracle database, and the Linux operating system on any hardware could offer a "best of breed" alternative to Microsoft's products. Negotiating revenue share would be an issue, but the three companies would have to compromise and figure out how to make the integrated product less expensive and better than the equivalent products from Microsoft.

Build a hosted application center

Given that the market is receptive to the idea of hosted applications, significant work would have to be done to set up an environment that can support users, applications, and data from a large number of businesses. Oracle would not be able to do this on its own. Perhaps in conjunction with IBM, Oracle could build an infrastructure reliable and scalable enough to make good on the promise of hosted applications. Both companies would have to compromise in some areas, but the combination could assemble functionality that would take Microsoft years to catch up.

Partner to win

Another area of potential partnerships for Oracle is to break into existing Microsoft strongholds. The strongest of Microsoft's partners today is Intel. And while Intel has enjoyed explosive growth due to its relationship with Microsoft, it has also been subject to the will of the software giant. During the response to the network computer challenge issued by Oracle, Intel was forced to almost half the price of its CPU semiconductors, while Microsoft barely changed the royalties associated with Windows. Microsoft forced much of the cost burden onto Intel, dramatically reducing Intel's margins and causing a big slip in the silicon provider's stock. Now is a good time for Oracle to approach Intel to work on projects and products that do not include Microsoft software. The development of information appliances for both businesses and consumers is a ripe opportunity, or they might focus on more forward-looking initiatives such as home networking or high-speed communications.

Oracle should not put any limits on the range of partners that it might work with to unseat Microsoft. Cellular phone manufacturers, as well as consumer electronics providers, are all meeting Oracle and Microsoft at the convergence of information and devices. Oracle has an opportunity to establish itself as the provider with vision and a sense of partnership to be selected to work on the next generation of exciting consumer and business products.

Offer an operating system

As Microsoft grows in power, the number of viable operating system choices available is becoming smaller and smaller. If the market were to arrive at a point where the only operating system options were available from Microsoft, Oracle may as well give up the database software business. Customers would default to buying a database from the same vendor that they buy the operating system from, and Microsoft could make SQL Server on Windows NT very well integrated while making it hard for Oracle to run its software on Windows NT. While operating system neutrality has long been a component of Oracle's strategic foundation, Oracle could meet Microsoft on Microsoft's own ground by offering an operating system of its own for free. There are some viable contenders in the market today, such as Linux, a free version of Unix that runs on a variety of hardware. An integrated offering of the Oracle database and an Oracle branded version of the Linux operating system would level the playing field against the integrated Microsoft Windows NT and Microsoft SQL Server combination.

Honing the Edge

The examples I've provided are just a handful of the possibilities available to and ahead of Oracle. More likely than any of them is the next revolutionary idea in Larry Ellison's head. But one thing is for sure. Oracle cannot continue on its current path and survive. Oracle is going to have to do something new, different, and extraordinary to take on the threat of Redmond.

Like Oracle, every company in a competitive market faces critical moments that determine whether the company will thrive or perish. And like Oracle, every businessperson must keep her eyes on future challengers as she positions her company for long-term success.

Not every company can double its revenues every year like Oracle did. And your company may not pass the billion dollar mark anytime soon. But every company—your company—can apply the lessons we've learned from the amazing growth and the hyper-competitive approach of the Oracle Corporation's success strategy.

Apply the fundamentals that Oracle uses to give your organization the Edge:

- Deliver products that you would use
- Build brand systematically
- Be first in a new market and dominate the market
- Foster entrepreneurship within the company
- Make your enemies' enemy your friend
- Guarantee success by developing new products for the "built-in consumer"
- Get the product out!
- Permeate the organization with information
- Build incredible selling power
- Talk with your customers; understand the issues
- Crush the competition
- Recruit athletes rather than experience
- Challenge the organization; teach people how to win
- Think like a shareholder
- Embrace change; it brings opportunity

It is truly an exciting time!

Index

A

Advanced services, 83–84
Advertising, 133–137
"Alexandria," 197
Amdahl, 4
Announcements, early product, 206–208
Apple Computer, Inc., 25, 32, 49, 197
Apple Macintosh, 41
Appliance devices, 231–232
Applications
    hosted, 226–228
    integrated, 229–231
    writing, 112
Ashton-Tate, 126, 135

B

Bell Atlantic, 196, 197
Benchmark performance, 111–112
Bennett, Rick, 136–137
Blythe Software, 31
Boot Camp, 107, 143, 150, 151, 152–156
British Telecom (BT), 196, 197, 198
Built-in customer concept, 54–56
Business, creating excitement about your, 18–22

C

CACI, 35, 37
Camaraderie, fostering, 70–71
CAP, 97–99
    paying price of, 186
Capital Cities/ABC complex, 197
Chief technical officer (CTO), 86–90
C language, 57–58, 59, 60
Classic product positioning, 131
Codd, E. F., 3–4, 131–132
College graduates, recruitment of, 143–150
Commercial database products, porting for, 57
Communicativeness in recruiting employees, 147

Company culture, indoctrinating employees with, 150–156
Compatibility, 156
Competition
    crushing, 121–140
    driving productivity with, 45–48
    eliminating, from your deals, 201–204
    presenting with problem for solving, 208–212
    steps attacking, 121–122
Competitive bulletins, 128–130
Competitive products, setup and, 29
Competitors
    documentation of victories over, 128–130
    lockout of, 138–140
    pigeonholing individual, 124–128
Compulsiveness in recruiting employees, 146–147
Computer platform
    choice of, 4
    making decisions about, 56–61
Connectability, 156
Consulting, 83
Cooperative Development Environment, 46
Core team, 67–71
Corporate standardization, 87–88
Cost, switching, 88
Cronkite, Walter, 197
Crucial issues, identifying, 184–190
Cullinet, 126–127
Customers
    explaining Oracle technology to prospective, 112
    focusing on care of, 189
    helping with product use, 109–115
    inclusion of, in product development, 105
    interaction with, 108–109
    lock in of, 138–140
    relationships with, 103–117
    talking with, 107–108
Customer support, putting regular employees on, 29

D

Data, migrating, 113–115
Database, laying out, 113
Database Forms, 72–73
Date, Chris, 131–132
Days Sales Outstanding (DSO), 99–100
dBase, 126, 135
Demonstrations, 89
Development, balancing, 39–41
Digital Equipment Corporation (DEC),
    56, 122, 127–128
Direct sales force, 223
Distributors' sales forces, assisting, 36
Dress code, 10–11

E

Education, 83
Electronic database, 5
Ellison, Larry
    and appreciation for Japanese art
        and culture, 11
    and consumer growth, 195
    and database concept, 205
    dress of, 10–11
    dubbing of Network Computer by,
        206
    gaining trust of, 41
    inspiring announcements from, 20
    intensiveness of, 16
    kernel team attention paid by, 70
    leadership of, 9–11
    as Oracle's visionary president, 5–6
    and perception of ownership, 17
    and perfection, 16–17
    persuasiveness of, 16
    reasons of, for Oracle's growth, 77
    and team decision on System R
        specification, 30
    vision of, 3–4, 25–26, 65–67
Employees
    giving opportunities to learn
        products, 28
    indoctrinating with company
        culture, 150–156
    inspiration of, 44

    putting regular, on customer
        support, 29
    rewarding, with stock options,
        69–71
Entrepreneurship, fostering, 41–45
Excitement Factor, 18–22
Executives, hiring of seasoned, 187–188
Expectations, setting realistic, 116–117

F

Field support engineers, 110–111, 111,
    114–115
Focus, maintaining, 44–45, 68
Franken, Al, 21
Functional Marketing, 136

G

Gain, Sybase's acquisition of, 32–33

H

Henley, Jeff, 187
Hewlett-Packard (HP), 56, 127–128
Hiring policies, 68–69, 187–188
Hosted application center, 233–234
Hosted applications, 226–228

I

IBM, 49, 56, 122, 127–128, 233
Icons, adopting, with relevant and
    positive associations, 11
Illustra, 33
Incentives for sales force, 78–81
Information, permeating organization
    with, 71–73
Information Management System
    (IMS), 5, 83
Informix, 19, 33, 48, 122–123, 125–126,
    128
Ingres, 19, 124, 132–133, 134
Integrated applications, 229–231
Intel, 234
Intelligence in recruiting employees, 146

Internal support for Oracle purchase, 89–90

International customers, adapting to needs of, 36–37

International headquarters for Oracle, 34–37

J

Java programming language, 49

Jobs, Steve, 10

K

Kellogg's, 30

Kernel group, 67–71

L

Lane, Ray, 187

Language variances, appreciating, 36

Lattice, 58

Layoffs, 190

Leadership, 9–11

Lessons, learning hard, 190–191

LJE Alert, 154

Local offices, establishing, 106

M

Management, maintaining visibility with top, 70

Management philosophy, 161–180

  accessibility of, 170–171

  giving power to individuals and teams, 163–166

  making and getting commitment, 167–168

  sales compensation system, 166–167

  spoiling best employees, 171–173

  teaching people how to win, 161–162

  think like shareholder, 169

Mantra, 156–158

Marketing, Functional, 136

Markets, exploring new, 193–213

Media Server, 197

Microsoft, 200–204

  clash between Oracle and, 5, 48–49, 217–221

  strengths of, 221–223

Microsoft Access, 42

Microsoft Windows NT, 202

Miner, Bob, 39–40, 43, 63

N

NCI, 180

Netscape Communications, 49, 233

Network computers, lessons learned from, 204–212

Network Product Division, 60

Network Products Division, 31

New products, creation of, 43–44

NeXT, 56

O

OASIS, 137

Object Linking and Embedding (OLE), 157–158

Object-oriented technology, 33, 40

Omnis, 31

Operating system dependent interface (ODI), 58

Opponents, fighting, on your terms, 130–133

Oracle, 3–4

  accounting at, 100

  acquisition of new technology products or companies by, 33–34

  Advanced Services group, 84

  advertising by, 133–137

  aggressiveness of sales products, 96–100

  alliances of, 48

  appliance devices, 231–232

  Applications group, 31, 180

  balance of development and sales at, 39–41

  beginnings of, 3–4

  benchmark performance at, 111–112

Boot Camp at, 107, 143, 150, 151, 152–156
and building of brand recognition, 30–31
built-in customer concept at, 54–56
character at, 9–22
clash between Microsoft and, 5, 48–49, 217–221
communicating success at, 13
communication of Mantra, 156–158
company culture, 18
consulting force, 224
continuous product release process, 65
core team, 67–71
corporate environment, 15
corporate strategy at, 25–49
creation of new products at, 43–44
and crushing competition, 121–140
and customer interaction, 108–109
customer relationships at, 103–117
customer service at, 29
customer support, 81–82
and customer use of products, 109–115
and database layout, 113
and data migration, 113–115
Days Sales Outstanding (DSO) at, 99–100
development team, 225–226
direct sales force, 223
and documentation of victories over competitors, 128–130
dress code at, 10–11
driving productivity with competition at, 45–48
and elimination of competition from deals, 201–204
employee consistency, 69
establishing local offices, 106
Excitement Factor at, 18–22
of executive briefing centers, 106
expertise, 225–226
explaining technology to prospective customer, 112

and exploration of new markets, 193–213
external market factor at, 77–78
field support engineers, 110–111, 111
and fixing of bugs, 111
fixing weaknesses, 191–192
focus at, 68
in forging partnerships, 233–235
fostering of entrepreneurship at, 41–45
freedom from PC, 225
future at, 217–236
"growth at all costs" doctrine, 183
growth of, 3, 31–34, 38, 53, 77, 82–83
handling product failures at, 61
hiring policies at, 68–69, 187–188
hosted applications, 226–228
hosting developer conferences, 106–107
hosting local seminars, 106–107
and identification of crucial issues, 184–190
implementation of systems using own software, 26–30
implementation of vertical sales force concept, 93–96
and inclusion of customers in product development, 105
indoctrination method, 150–156
infrastructure at, 81–86
installed base, 224–225
integrated applications, 229–231
international headquarters for, 34–37
intolerance for mediocrity, 17
investigation of computer products, 29
layoffs at, 190
leadership at, 9–11
learning hard lessons, 190–191
and lessons learned from network computer, 204–212
lock in of customers by, 138–140
lockout of competition by, 138–140

maintaining of focus at, 44–45

marketing of, to enterprise customers, 90–92

name for, 30–31

Network Product Division, 60

New Media group at, 180, 196, 198–200

office space for, 11–14

and opportunity for change, 179–180

permeation of, with organization, 71–73

personnel recruitment philosophy, 143–150

philosophy at, 6

and pigeonholing of individual competitions by, 124–128

and portability, 53, 59–60

potential of, 77

pricing at, 229

product announcements at, 20–21

product development at, 53–73

product development team, 61

and production of annual report on CD-ROM, 29–30

product quality at, 179

promotion of vision at, 100–102

providing enterprise applications, 224

quality control as, 226

realistic expectations at, 116–117

regional sales at, 94

relational database model of, 5

revenues at, 3, 6, 67

rewarding employees with stock options, 69–71

sales efforts at, 212–213

sales force at, 78–81

sales incentives at, 79–80

selling power, 77–102

seminars of, 90–92

sending employees to trade shows to demonstrate, 28

shipping history, 64–65

standards at, 6

strategies that amplify advantages, 226–232

strengths of, 223–226

subsidiaries of, 38–39

talent at, 144–158

and talking with customers, 107–108

teaching classes using, 27–28

technical training at, 111

turn around of, 186–190

universality in vision of, 3–4

use of own products by, 26

User Group at, 116–117

value of employees at, 44

vision at, 25–26, 65–66, 66–67

writing of applications by, 112

yearly reorganization at, 175–179

Oracle for Macintosh, 42

Oracle Forms, 31

Oracle 8i, 43, 226

Oracle Media Objects, 30

Oracle purchase, internal support for, 89–90

Oracle SQL*Calc, 32

P

Pacific Gas & Electric, 25, 32

Parking lost test, 12

Peddersen, Tom, Associates, 34, 37

Personnel recruitment philosophy at Oracle, 143–150

Point of Pressure, 86–90

Portability, 59–60, 156

Porting, 59

    for commercial database products, 57

Positive perception, projecting, 11–13

Presales, 85–86

Price, selling, 87

Problemsolving and competition, 208–212

Product development, 53–73

    inclusion of customers in, 105

Product implementation barrier, 138–139

Productivity, driving, with competition, 45–48
Products
early announcements of, 206–208
helping customers with, 109–115
portability of, 53
quality of, 179
using own, 26
Product switching barrier, 139–140

R

Red Packet, 72
Regional sales, 94
Relational database model, 5
Relational technology, 116
"Release early, release often" principle, 64
Revenues, booking, 184–185
Rundgren, Todd, 197

S

Sales, 212–213
balancing, 39–41
Sales force
incentives for, 78–81
vertical, 93–96
Sega, 197
Selling power, 77–102
Selling price, 87
Seminars, 90–92
Sense of humor, in recruiting
employees, 147
Software, implementing systems using
your, 26–30
Software Development Laboratories, 30
Soviet Union, 38
SQL★ architecture, 100–103
SQL★Forms, 55–56, 100
SQL★Loader product, 140
SQL★ Report, 100
Stock options, 69–71
Strategic Business Units (SBUs), 45
Structured Query Language (SQL), 4
Style, designing with, 13–14
Success, communicating, 13

Sun Microsystems, 49, 233
Switching cost, 88
Sybase, 19, 48, 124–125, 135–136
acquisition of Gain in, 32–33
"System R" specification, 4, 30
Systems Network Architecture (SNA),
102

T

Talent, 144–158
Target market, focusing on, 97
Team mystique, promoting, 70
Telesales, 84–85
Time differences, accounting for, 35
Trade shows
sending people to, 28
training employees in product use
at, 28
Transaction, 62–63

U

United Airlines, 105
Universality in vision of Oracle, 4
User Group meetings, 116–117
USWest, 196, 197

V

Vertical industries, selling, 93–96
Vertical sales force, implementation of,
93–96
Vision, promoting, 100–102

W

WhiteSmith, 58

Selling Microsoft

by Doug Dayton

S E L L I N G
MICROSOFT

SALES SECRETS FROM
INSIDE THE WORLD'S MOST
SUCCESSFUL COMPANY

DOUG DAYTON

Trade paperback, 1-58062-052-3
272 pages, $9.95

Microsoft insider Doug Dayton shows you the innovative sales tactics that helped drive the company to its unprecedented "total domination" of the personal computer software market—and how you can use the same techniques to increase your own sales! In *Selling Microsoft*, Doug Dayton shares his powerful, unique sales system—known as, "Client-Centered Selling"—that helped him transform the OEM sales organization into one of the most successful and effective in the business.

Also available from Adams Media Corporation

The Marketing Game

by Eric Schulz

INSIDER STRATEGIES AND TECHNIQUES
FROM TODAY'S MARKETING LEADERS

THE MARKETING GAME

How the World's
Best Companies Play to Win

ERIC SCHULZ
FORMER MARKETING EXECUTIVE FOR

PROCTER & GAMBLE
THE WALT DISNEY COMPANY
THE COCA-COLA COMPANY

Hardcover, 1-58062-222-4
304 pages, $24.95

The Marketing Game breaks the code of silence to teach you the covert strategies and secrets of the world's most savvy marketers. Whether you own a small delicatessen or are employed at a multi-national corporation, *The Marketing Game* will work for you. You'll learn in a clear and straightforward way how easy it is to outsmart your competitor.

STUART READ is a seven-year veteran of Oracle Corporation, as a Senior Director of the New Media Group, Director of Network Products, and Group Product Manager. A graduate in Computer Science of Harvard University, he has also worked at Lotus Development Corporation, Sun Microsystems, and software startups Avistar and Diba, Inc. He is currently the vice president of marketing at AvantGo, Inc. and lives in Portola Valley, in northern California.